LINDA PIERCE PICCIOTTO

LEARNING
TOGETHER

A Whole Year
In A
Primary Classroom

Scholastic Canada Ltd.

To my family, Charly, Carl and Sarah,
and to Mary,
as she begins her own teaching career

Scholastic Canada Ltd.
123 Newkirk Road, Richmond Hill, Ontario, Canada L4C 3G5

Scholastic Inc.
730 Broadway, New York, NY 10003, USA

Ashton Scholastic Limited
Private Bag 1, Penrose, Auckland, New Zealand

Ashton Scholastic Pty Limited
PO Box 579, Gosford, NSW 2250, Australia

Scholastic Publications Ltd.
Villiers House, Clarendon Avenue, Leamington Spa, Warwickshire CV32 5PR, UK

Cover design by Yüksel Hassan, background photo © by Digital Images/Firstlight, classroom photo by Christine Dunsmoor.

6 5 4 3 2 1   Printed in Canada   3 4 5 6 7/9

Canadian Cataloguing in Publication Data

Picciotto, Linda Pierce
  Learning together

Includes bibliographical references.
ISBN 0-590-74712-6

1. Elementary school teaching. I. Title.

LB1507.P53 1993   372.11'02   C93-094550-6

CONTENTS

Introduction 1
   Overview of the book 1
   My class 2
   My beliefs about learning and teaching 4

Basic organization 10
   Records 10
      Forms 10
      Binder 11
   Classroom management 13
      Tables 13
      Totes 14
      Writing workshop folders 14
      Notebooks 14
      Sorters 14
      Calendar 15
      "Magnetic students" 15
      Chance box 16
      Listening center 16
      Class newsletters 16
   Interest studies 17
      Major interest studies 17
      Minor interest studies 18

The program and evaluation 19
   A general outline 19
   A closer look at the outline 21
      Daily 21
      Two or three times a week 30
      Weekly 31
      Often throughout the year 33

A whole year of learning together 35
   My plan for the year 35
   How the year unfolded 36
      Safety 36
      Tadpoles 42

Kyla 42
Cooking 44
Thanksgiving 45
Halloween 47
A house in the street 49
Art gallery trip 50
Salmon 50
Student-led conferences 52
Plant growth 53
Hanukkah 55
A taste of Japan 57
The winter concert 57
Science experiments 59
Polar bears 62
Valentine's Day 64
Chinese New Year 65
Castles 66
Mother's Day 69
Father's Day 70
Happy notes for the principal 71
Egg incubation 72
The museum 73
Parent Appreciation Tea 73
Our class annual 74
Family camping trip 75
Beach trip 75
Games Day 75
Four days in detail 76
Afterword 78
A note to new teachers 79
Bibliography 83
Index 84

INTRODUCTION

Overview of the book

This is a book about teaching, written out of my 15 years of experience. It describes my own teaching in a primary classroom: how I organize daily, weekly and occasional activities so my students can develop skills and grow in knowledge while becoming increasingly independent learners. It describes how I combine a variety of major and minor interest studies with routine activities to give the students a rich, interesting and balanced program.

I didn't start out teaching in the way the book describes. Like many traditional teachers, I had difficulty imagining how an integrated, "child-centered" program would work. How could such a program possibly give children the skills they need? How would I keep track of what they were learning? How would I ever have enough ideas to keep things interesting and running smoothly? How would I organize my classroom, my schedule, my reporting?

It hadn't taken me long to become dissatisfied with traditional approaches. I was pleased with my early attempts to make changes in my teaching, and my move to "whole language" teaching happened rather quickly. As my beliefs and practices matured, I felt increasingly better about my teaching. Now my students love to come to school. Generally they are happily and productively involved in their work, and their parents are pleased to see them excited about learning.

I often hear my earlier doubts expressed by others. They find it difficult to understand how a holistic classroom works. Reading educational philosophy isn't enough. What does "Let the children use their own ideas" *really* mean? Won't there be chaos in the classroom? Won't the parents be confused? Won't I lose track of where the children are in their development?

I hope this book will help to answer some of those questions. The contents are organized as follows:

- In the rest of the introduction I briefly describe my classroom and outline my beliefs about teaching and learning.

- In the first chapter I describe some practical organization and management techniques I've found useful for maintaining a successful program.

- The following chapter focuses on the routine classroom and school activities that form the backbone of my program. There I describe how both the students and their parents are involved in the program, and how I work a variety of evaluation procedures into the schedule.

- ◆ Chapter three consists of three connected parts: an outline of my plans for one full year, a description of how I changed and adapted those plans as the students and I came to know each other and enjoyed shared experiences, and a graphic depiction of how my daily routines are integrated with major and minor interest studies.
- ◆ Finally, in the afterword, I add a note of reassurance for beginning teachers.

As completely as I can, I've described the events in my classroom during one school year. This is how I teach. This is what works best for me.

We all have our own styles and personalities, of course, and none of us can claim to have the "one best way." We teach in different communities with diverse school populations and unique parent and administrative expectations. Our students learn in many ways and thrive in many different classroom environments. We can learn from each other, however. We shouldn't all have to invent the same wheels. What works for one teacher may also work for another, with a few modifications to suit a different teaching style and a different classroom situation.

I've tried to make the descriptions of my teaching detailed enough to be of help to new teachers in particular. I hope they'll be of interest to more experienced teachers as well.

My class

I teach in a school with about 200 students in grades K-7. Our parents expect to be involved in their children's schooling. My fellow teachers and I are responsible for our own programs, but we receive a lot of help from the parents, and we share some of the decision-making with them.

Since our school believes in multi-age grouping, all classes contain at least two age groups. Most children have the same teacher for two years, but the classes change: at the end of each year about half the students move to another class and half stay with their current teacher. The children who stay know the routines and expectations and are eager to help the newcomers adjust, so we can begin implementing our programs much earlier in the year than is possible when the entire class is new. Establishing communication with the new parents is also easier.

The benefits for both "old-timers" and "newcomers" are substantial. The system encourages students to become more independent. In a mixed-age group, everyone — students, parents and teacher — *expects* the children to be at many different developmental levels academically, socially and emotionally. This encourages a "family" feeling, with all members of the class supportive of each other at whatever level they may be, in all areas of the curriculum.

Observation

"'pet?'"
    "Yes, Amy, it's time to sit on the carpet."

"'ter ear."

"Your new baby sister is here? Oh yes, there she is with your mom. She's sleeping! How is she?"

"'ine."

After carpet time, Michelle, our speech therapist, appeared and asked to see Amy.

"Amy, would you like to go with Michelle for a few minutes?"

"Daw."

"You can draw when you come back."

"No, daw." Tears formed.

"Oh dear, Michelle, she's afraid to go with you. Could she take a friend?"

"Of course."

"Barbara, would you like to go with Amy? She doesn't want to go by herself."

Barbara recognized the difficulty and was happy to help out. The year before she'd been quite shy herself in this class. She took Amy by the hand and they followed Michelle for the beginning of a series of much-needed speech lessons. Now, every time Amy sees Michelle coming into the room on Tuesday afternoons, she goes to find Barbara.

Barbara tells me that the lessons are interesting, and that it's becoming easier to understand Amy. I think so too, and Amy's parents are very pleased — and Barbara's mom is happy that her daughter has an important job at school.

As Amy is very young in many ways, she may stay in my early primary class for an extra year. Her parents and I will make that decision together when the time comes. My program is flexible enough to allow her to experience success at school and to benefit from her contact with her friends and teachers.

Generally we move children to a new class only in September, and then we carefully consider academic, social, emotional and physical factors. Our goals are to place each child in the learning environment most appropriate for him or her and to create heterogeneous groups that work well together.

I teach the very youngest children in the school. Of the roughly 25 students, about half — the kindergarteners — attend only in the afternoons (1:00-3:00) and all day on Wednesdays (8:45-1:45). Wednesday is a short day in our school, with the afternoon reserved for professional development. So, on four mornings each week I'm able to give the senior students a lot of individual attention, which is important at this stage of their schooling. The following year, of course, my "half-day" students will have the advantage of being in this small morning group. Our students don't experience a big jump between kindergarten and grade one, since the half-day students are already well integrated into the school routines.

At 1:00 PM I meet with the new arrivals for "carpet time" while the others enjoy quiet "table time." Afterwards comes a variety of activities, depending on the day: "activity time," music lessons, library visits, gym time, outside playtime and so forth. The older children participate in all of these activities with their younger peers, according to their personal levels of development.

Observation

The first week of school each all-day child is appointed to be official "special helper" for a new, usually nervous half-day student. The helpers give their charges a tour of the school (including the restrooms!) and stay close by them at recess time and on field trips or walks to the school library. The helper ties shoes, searches for lost jackets and in general provides comfort. Not only does this make the teacher's job much easier, it also makes the little ones feel more secure. The older students feel needed and have a chance to demonstrate responsibility. Classroom routines are quickly learned when there are so many teachers!

My beliefs about learning and teaching

I believe that children should enjoy school and learning.

I want my students to feel good about themselves as learners and as individuals. I want to help them grow intellectually, emotionally and physically.

I believe that I can accomplish that basic goal in a holistic classroom — if I know exactly what it is I'm trying to do!

My teaching may look to some, at first, like an unplanned "do your own thing" approach. Actually, however, it has an underlying structure that is well understood by my administrators, my fellow teachers, the children's parents and, at a different level, the children themselves. For my program to be successful, I must:

◆ be thoroughly familiar with the *curriculum* I am trusted to teach, the *skills* the students need in order to become successful learners, and the *range of experiences* I must provide to ensure a proper balance;

◆ be familiar with *different learning styles* and create programs varied enough to give individual students opportunities to work in ways that are most efficient and enjoyable for them;

◆ know about *child development* so I can predict what is likely to occur next and plan activities that will facilitate growth in the different areas of the curriculum.

I believe that my program must be balanced.

I need to include a variety of activities that will allow my students to work in different ways and with many different people, to learn a variety of things, and to explore the world outside the school. I want to help the children know how much there is to learn "out there" and how to go about learning it.

Students also need a balance of directed, individual and cooperative activities. They need a balance of "input" and "output" times during the day, and as many hands-on experiences as possible. Gone are the days when learning about science or other subjects meant copying paragraphs from the board.

I believe that all students should be able to work at levels appropriate for them and be encouraged to progress at their own rates.

This does not mean that students never hear discussions that are "above their heads" or that they are never involved in lessons dealing with concepts that are more appropriate for more mature students. Such experiences are good for them. When a new child is welcomed into a family, the parents don't abandon the more advanced books they've begun to read to their older children; the new child listens too, and enjoys the experience at his or her own level.

Similarly, more mature students benefit from repetition of some of the concepts their younger classmates are being taught. Working with and helping their less-advanced peers helps them consolidate their own learning and fosters the development of their self-esteem.

I don't distribute worksheets that might be appropriate for six students, too easy for 10, and too difficult for another 10. Nor do I divide my students into groups and label them. Instead, I present a good variety of open-ended assignments that can be completed by all students according to their abilities and interests. I have different expectations for each child and form groups using criteria other than academic levels.

I believe it's important for children to be aware of their own development and that of their peers.

I try to teach my students to be empathetic. They need to understand that people grow in different ways and at different rates and times. They need to understand that "quicker" or "sooner" isn't necessarily "better" or "smarter." They need to be supportive of their classmates who are at different levels, who learn in different ways or who have different needs. And they shouldn't be hard on themselves if they are among the late developers or slower thinkers. If children have experienced that the comments of their peers are usually positive and helpful, they'll feel free to show and discuss their work and express their opinions. My goal is for all children to see themselves as learners.

Being empathetic towards each other at school is a first step to being empathetic towards different people in the world. I hope to build attitudes in the classroom that will last a lifetime.

I believe that deliberate modeling is important for students.

Teachers have always modeled, without thinking much about it. I believe that I should be very aware of the modeling I'm doing, however, and of its importance. My students need to see me writing well-constructed sentences, paragraphs and, in later years, reports. They need to hear me reading and discussing books with enthusiasm. They need to see both me and their peers working with numbers, and to share the excitement of discovering patterns and understanding concepts.

All students need to have contact with adults and other children who are excited about what they are learning and who are eager to share their knowledge. They need to watch others learning and take part in the process. I don't plan an entire unit and present my students with the finished product. I involve them by suggesting that they visit the library for books and asking them to help me decide what speakers to invite and what field trips to plan. I encourage them to ask their parents for ideas that might be useful in our information gathering as well.

***I believe that the attitudes I display and the environment I establish set the
learning tone in the classroom.***

It's important for me to ask questions with many possible answers. My students need
to know that there are different ways of looking at problems or issues. I try to lead
discussions and plan activities that will help them develop the ability to think clearly
and creatively and to analyze situations and statements critically. I encourage them
to do more and more of the questioning themselves.

I work to create a stimulating, interesting, changing and child-centered
environment. I set up my classroom in such a way that supplies and educational
materials of all kinds can be easily seen and reached, and I organize these materials
so that, after a bit of training (and constant reminders), they can be kept in order by
the students without my help or direction.

Some things in the room stay the way we first set them up: the book corner (with
a regular replacement of books, of course), the tape recorder and its accompanying
collection of tapes and read-along books, the math manipulative shelves, the art
supply and junk box corner, the filing cabinet, the guinea pig cage. However, other
things are being added and removed all the time — by me, by the students and by
their parents. Almost nothing goes on my bulletin boards that isn't made or brought
in by students. There's a place for other things, such as professional art work, as
well, but I don't care for teacher-store art, like clowns holding balloons with the
names of the colors, so they don't make it past my censorship. I have to live in the
room too!

***I believe that students must be given a good deal of decision-making power, both
in their individual work and in the running of the class.***

My students know I'm in charge, but they also know that it's *their* class —
everyone's, not just mine. Everyone must take responsibility for the learning and
socializing that goes on in the classroom, and for the maintenance of an orderly,
efficient learning environment.

Allowing the students to make decisions doesn't mean I never ask them to
participate in an activity or complete an assignment they think they won't enjoy.
They are not yet capable of taking complete charge of their learning programs or of
balancing their own needs with those of the others in the class.

Observation

When I ask my students to do something, I usually take the time to explain the reasons.
Children comply with requests more readily if they understand why those requests are
being made, and individuals often discover that they enjoy or learn from activities they
first disliked or feared.

"Please put that whistle away, Ellen. Your friends can't concentrate well when you make
that noise, and I find it difficult to teach."

"Please move away from Ted, Eric, and turn your body so you're facing the board. This is
a very important lesson and you need to listen carefully."

"I know you'd rather stay inside to finish your picture, Polly, but we're all going outside now and I can't leave you alone . . . and we all need the fresh air."

"You may work with the pattern blocks in a minute, Carl, but first I'd like you to finish this counting activity with Sarah."

I believe that the best teachable moments often occur unexpectedly.

I keep a globe and map close at hand so we can locate places when we see or hear them mentioned in our reading or discussions. If there's a house being moved in the area, if an apartment building is going up nearby, or if a visitor from some interesting place is in the school, I take advantage of the educational opportunities these real events present.

I take for granted and capitalize on the children's natural curiosity and enthusiasm when I make my plans. The amount of time we spend on a topic depends on their interest in it, as well as on the necessity of maintaining a balanced program.

I believe that art should play a strong role in any program.

I schedule enough time during the day for my students to become really involved with art. I expose them to many types of professional art in many different settings, encourage them to try a variety of techniques and materials, and see that they have a wide range of art experiences. This kind of focusing helps them to become more observant.

```
Robert   🖼 ✏ |  🎨 🖼 🐱
        I like drawing.  It is one one of my
favourite activities.  I gave Michael and Thomas
drawing lessons.  I learned how to draw well
last year.  I draw all the time.
```

Beyond that, however, I don't interfere with their art. Children are natural artists and express themselves in wonderfully diverse ways when given the opportunity. Teacher-directed art projects — assembling objects using adult-drawn designs, copying pictures drawn by someone else, coloring worksheets — have no place in my classroom. My students have their own ideas and work with great concentration to complete projects that come from their own imagination and experience. When their artwork is displayed on the walls of the classroom and in the halls, they know it's valued. As a result, they grow in self-esteem. Most children who experience enjoyment and success in their art will continue to produce original, interesting works throughout their elementary school careers — perhaps throughout their lives.

Observation

The art that Armando completed during writing workshop time was unremarkable. His father had taught him how to draw a man and he generally drew variations of this figure dressed in different clothes and brandishing different weapons.

One beautiful day I gave the children boards, pencils and paper for some drawing on the playground. I asked them to choose something to sketch. They could draw anything they wished — the swing set, the blue elephant slide, a bush, one of the rocks, anything that caught their attention.

That day I discovered that Armando has a special talent in art. He seated himself at the base of our very tall cedar tree and looked up into the branches. The line drawing he completed was stunning. His sense of proportion was wonderful. In the tree was a figure climbing. He said, "That's me." He had really "gotten into" the tree.

When we borrowed a mounted bat from the museum to do some sketches at Halloween time, Armando created another very beautiful line drawing. Afterwards I noticed that he began to choose a wider variety of subjects during writing workshop time and art periods. These successes had helped him grow in self-confidence.

Observation

JoAnne, a friend of Amy's mother, is an artist. When I invited her to come into the classroom to show us her work, she brought in slides and some framed prints. The children watched the slides with great interest, asked her questions and told her what they saw in her paintings. At the end of the short show, the students had a chance to do some artwork themselves.

I suggested that they might use some of the themes JoAnne had used: hearts, borders, repeated symbols and geometric shapes. Kate seemed especially inspired. She created a painting that was quite unlike anything she had ever produced before. All her classmates commented on its special qualities. Perhaps the next artist we invite into our classroom will inspire a different child.

Observation

We took a trip to the art gallery to see a special collection by Canadian painters. The children were given an opportunity to do some sketches while they were there, but the results weren't too interesting because they hadn't had enough time and the colored pencils and cheap newsprint provided by the Gallery didn't allow them to create work that was memorable. They did enjoy the paintings and sculptures they saw there, however, and the teachers helped them to see things they might not have seen by themselves.

Back in the classroom I spread out reproductions of paintings that were part of a set from the media center. We looked at them and discussed them briefly, and I asked the students to tell about a part of one painting they especially liked. Then I handed out white paper and new felt pens. I didn't suggest that they copy any of the paintings, but some of the children used ideas from them.

Robert asked for a very large piece of paper. He put it on the floor near the painting easel and proceeded to make a variety of marks on it with many different colors. It was quite unlike any of his other drawings: he usually created very detailed scenes of knights in armor or cowboys and towns in the Old West.

"Does your painting have a name?" I asked him.

"No," he replied. "It's an abstract."

Sonja used many of the design elements from one of the paintings she liked. Her painting was bold and beautifully balanced in form and in color. Her parents framed it.

I believe that the whole school should become a community.

It's important for all the teachers in a school to communicate with each other about their programs so the children's total school experience will be balanced. The students in different classes need to have contact with each other as well, and with other teachers. Children are usually interested in what other students are doing. I've found that the transition from one level to another is smoother for those students who have had some contact with the next level during the year. In our school we deliberately try to organize a variety of contacts. Our weekly "buddy time" activities are quite special to the children, for instance, and both senior and junior buddies look forward to their time together.

Sometimes the four primary teachers arrange a series of "bridging" days when our combined classes form mixed groups that circulate, on a specific schedule, to all four classrooms. One year we set up a different craft in each room in December and a different science experiment in each room in January. In March Christine organized a special art project in her room, Karen taught a new game in the gym, Marg planned an interesting math activity and I monitored partner reading.

Sometimes the entire school is involved in a study such as astronomy, the ocean or Native Peoples. We are careful not to overdo these massive studies, however, since they take a lot of energy and limit the flexibility of each class. We all want to give our students enough time to pursue their own interests in their own ways.

We are always delighted by the informal contacts that are made as well.

♦ Four students from Karen's class performed a play for us.

♦ We went to see Karen's students' clay fish and their newly hatched salmon.

♦ Marg's class came to see the playhouse castle we made.

♦ Sarah, a student from Christine's class, popped in to ask if they could share their artwork with us. We dropped what we were doing and went over to enjoy the still-wet murals of a walk they had taken in the park.

♦ Christine and I decided to combine our small morning classes to watch a video about beetles. Afterwards we helped every student find a partner from the other class, and each pair painted wonderful giant insects that we displayed in the hall between our rooms.

Experiences like these serve to enrich the lives of our students and make them feel more at ease in the school as a whole. Moving to a new classroom in September won't be a big deal: they've been there before, lots of times, and they already know their new teacher.

Robert

the taoll hhap is flering a cKanin.
It is clld the fai egoll.

BASIC ORGANIZATION

Records

Since I plan to make many observations and take many notes during the school year, I make sure that I have a well-organized system of evaluation in place before the year begins, so my data gathering will be easy and systematic. The following system works well for me.

Forms

I use a series of forms I designed. (See *Evaluation: A Team Effort* for more details.)

Class list forms

After my class enrolment has been established, I write the students' names in alphabetical order in the left-hand column of three different forms (variously spaced for different purposes). Then I photocopy them in three different colors and three-hole punch them for ready use when I need them.

Form 1 — "Reading – Daily News"

"Barbara brought in her black and white striped cat this morning. It didn't really like to be at school...."

Subject: Reading – Daily News   Date: March 15

Students:

- **Amy** — pointed to words l—r but not following voice as she tried to remember 'news' (B's cat was here today...")
- **Armando** — pointer followed words well – clear he is beginning to use init. cons. When knew he omitted a word he looked at whole word + often knew!
- **Barbara** — Fluent, good expression. Could tell me why 'the' is in didn't
- **Carl** — read slowly, word by w, but w/o great difficulty. s/c "stripped" to "striped"
- Carol
- Christop[her]
- Ellen
- Eric
- Jamie
- Janet
- Jerry
- Kate

Form 2 — "Activity Time"

Subject: Activity Time

© = cooperative play/work
Ⓐ = associative
Ⓢ = solitary

Date: April 3

Students:

- **Amy** — Ⓢ felts / Ⓢ book - "read" out loud / Ⓐ felts - chatting w/color
- **Armando** — © water table - measuring, pouring - "we scientists" - w/ Eric, Jerry, Barbara
- **Barbara** — © zoo Armando
- **Carl** — © Lego - built a zoo, incl. animals - w/ Jamie
- **Carol** — Ⓐ felt pen drawings - group making cards - Ellen, Polly, Ted, ... Amy too
- **Christopher** — © playhouse w/Mich..., Robert, Ryan
- Eric

Form 3 — "Project Day" group work

After long walk in Beacon Hill Park

Subject: "Project Day" group work   Date: May 18

Students in Groups:

- **Amy / Janet / Michael / Ryan** — Conference – all gave ideas – decided on painted mural of pond – good coop to get supplies – Kind but firm w/Amy when she painted trees from other side.. made her turn them into clouds + start from other side – OK w/ her. Good sharing of materials, supportive comments to all, all kept w/ it. Easy finished on time + were proud of results. Easy clean up.
- **Ellen / Jamie / Barbara / Ted** — Ⓔ took charge – decided they'd do a "duck play – puppets" OK. w/ J + B, Ⓣ wanted to build an adventure playground w/blocks, but yielded. All made puppet ducks w/ toilet p. rolls – Ⓔ thought of design, others followed. Ⓣ made scenery but Ⓔ not satisfied – came to me – & said talk to him + she did – ok then – he added to it. Ⓔ set up puppet theatre. All participated in performance – plotless but enjoyed by all. Cute ducks!
- **Carol / Christopher** — Ⓜ suggested a model of the playground. All agreed. Used art box junk – © swings, Ⓡ teeter-totters Ⓡ slide ⓨ base for all, bushes around edges. Helped each other w/design problems (swings didn't start – Ⓡ got plasticine Happy group – suppor...

Student cards

To organize notes about individual students I use a legal-size file folder with overlapping library book pockets glued inside for holding small, labeled cards for each student.

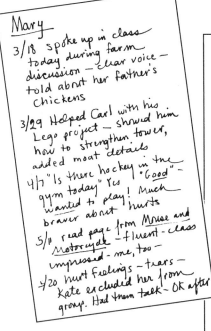

Individual student files

The top drawer of my filing cabinet contains a set of file folders, one for each student, stapled along the edges so small pieces of paper won't be lost. Into these go copies of report cards, notes from parents (including the formal evaluations I've asked them to complete), permission slips, any of my own comments that I consider too personal to put where they might be seen by others, notes or drawings given to me by the children and anything else I want to keep. Some of this material will be transferred to the students' cumulative files at the end of the year and passed on to their next year's teacher.

Binder

As a place to keep my own notes, records and plans I use a large three-ring binder with dividers marking the following sections:

Calendar

In this section I put a copy of the school calendar so I can keep track of meetings and special events. To these I add the dates of our own class activities.

Year plan

This section holds my long-range planning, with notes for my different interest studies. Some notes I make after class discussions, some while planning joint studies with a fellow teacher or the entire staff, some when I think of something that will provide balance to a particular interest study. Ideas from parents also make their way into this section. I record things I need to purchase or borrow, material I need to assemble and people I need to speak with, and I sketch out rough schedules.

Daily plans

For this section I photocopy day-of-the-week sheets for recording my schedules for recess, lunch, gym, music, library and assistant time so I can work around those times when I plan. I also fill in special events, like field trips, from the calendar section to give myself double reminders. I generally put about three months worth of these daily sheets in my binder at one time, removing outdated ones to a file folder so the section won't be too bulky.

I confess that my notes on these daily sheets are sketchy, and often I don't even use them. New teachers will probably want to, but my experience and approach have given me the confidence to do a lot of planning in my head. I also want the flexibility to be able to change my plans when I realize that something else might be more effective, or when my students' interest has been attracted by another topic that has learning potential.

Class lists

This section consists of a list of my students with their birthdates and the names, addresses and telephone numbers of their parents or guardians.

Parents

The parent section has lists of things individuals are willing to do to assist me and the children in or out of the classroom. I also keep notes for and minutes of the bi-monthy family meetings that take place in a parent's home, and notes from meetings with my two class coordinators, parent volunteers who coordinate parent assistance for me and help me maintain good parent communication.

Staff lists

This section contains the names, addresses and phone numbers of all my colleagues at school, specialists (with their schedules) and members of the administration and the media center — anyone I may need to contact for some special purpose. It also contains a list of teachers on call for those days when I can't be in my classroom.

School meetings

This section is reserved for the minutes of our monthly staff meetings and committees.

Out-of-school contacts

Here I record a list of names and phone numbers of the people or organizations I've contacted or plan to contact for such things as arranging field trips or visits to our school. Since it's easy to misplace this type of information, it's convenient to have it all in one place for quick answers to organizational questions: "Where did we buy those fertile eggs last year?"

Budget

I keep track of what I've spent for the classroom from the various funds I have at my disposal. I also keep track of what I've ordered and mark off items when they've been delivered. I also make a note of any items I'd like to order, even if I don't have the funds at the moment. Maybe in the future . . .

Classroom management

If I want my students to manage certain procedures independently and take responsibility for keeping the room and their belongings in order, I need to take the time and make the effort to provide facilities, organize carefully, explain clearly and *monitor diligently* until I'm sure good habits have been established.

There's nothing new about my system of classroom management. Good management is a matter of establishing patterns that become automatic for everyone. Students are capable of doing more for themselves than we used to think possible, and in a holistic classroom it's essential that they become independent and responsible.

The following set of management systems work well for me. Not discussed in detail below, but also important, are procedures for:

- book storage
- the management of student portfolios (collections of their important papers)
- the use of the computer and the storing of disks
- the organization of math and art materials, coats and boots . . .
- the use of the school library

I try to make my expectations very clear concerning behavior in the classroom, the halls, the gym and the playground, and on field trips — as well as the consequences for students who choose to ignore the rules!

Tables

I prefer five or six round tables instead of individual desks. Tables provide much more flexibility, allowing work areas to be changed easily. I can also change seating arrangements quickly to meet immediate social or academic needs by putting name cards on the tables to indicate where the children are to work. In this way I can encourage all students to interact with many different classmates and still make sure that those who don't manage well together stay separated. Sometimes the students choose their own places, but they know that I'll ask them to move if their arrangement interferes with their learning.

Totes

The children all have rectangular plastic totes that are stored in labeled cubbyholes in a cabinet. In their totes they keep small personal belongings, school supplies and projects under construction, all the things normally kept in a desk. These totes are portable: if a project is being completed in the hall, the necessary supplies simply go along. Totes are easier for children to keep tidy than desk space. Larger items such as books are kept under the totes.

Writing workshop folders

I prepare individual file folders for my students, each one clearly marked with the child's name. These I place in alphabetical order in a special drawer of my filing cabinet. I teach the students to place their daily date-stamped writing workshop papers behind those already in their files, so they'll be kept in order.

Notebooks

I create a notebook for each student, using plain three-hole paper for younger students and paper on which I've photocopied a few widely spaced lines at the bottom for older students. It's easy to collect art and writing samples by distributing these notebooks once a week and asking the students to do their writing workshop in the notebook on that day. No gathering, sorting and selecting stray papers! These notebooks are very useful during student-led conferences and report card writing time.

Sorters

That's what I call the organizers I make to keep the students' papers separate and ready to take home. I make two, each with half as many dividers as there are students in the class, since they are easier to handle with just 12 or 13 sections. I staple dividers (each one slightly longer than the one before) together at the bottom, inside a file folder. Then I write the children's names, one on each divider, in alphabetical order. Into these sorters go school newsletters and notices and any personal notes I've written to the parents. The students may insert their own work as well, as long as it's relatively flat. At the end of the day I call the names and distribute the material. With this system I'm sure that papers are saved for any students who are absent (they simply stay in the sorter), and I don't have to deal with unwieldy piles of loose notices and student work.

Observation

"Nice drawing, Amy. Do you want to take it home?"
  "Yes."
"Then put it into your sorter so you won't forget it."
Amy looked at me. It was clear she didn't know what I was talking about.
"You know — there near the door. Find your own name in the red sorter."
Amy shook her head. Impossible. So I went with her.
"There. See the big 1? Your name is in that folder. Can you find it?"
Amy shook her head.
"It's the third one. See the letters? It says *Amy*. Look. I'll put a red star next to your name so you can find it next time. OK?"
  "OK."
"Just lift up the divider with the star and put your drawing under it."
  "OK."
Amy smiled. She was proud. She had taken another step towards independence. Now she could use the sorter like everyone else.

Calendar

We have a number of daily calendar routines:

◆ Print the current date on a square of paper and clip it onto the calendar.
◆ Update the "days of the week" cards.
◆ Read the thermometer, print the number on a card and lead the "guess the temperature" game.
◆ Gather the magnetized weather cards for discussing the weather in French.

Sometimes other jobs are added, at my suggestion or a student's. For instance, one year they wanted to take turns calling the roll. The students and I developed a system to keep track of the turns, to save time and avoid arguments.

"Magnetic students"

I noticed "magnetic students" while visiting University Hill Elementary School in Vancouver. I precut tagboard heads (about 5 cm high) and give one to each student to draw a face and print his or her name at the bottom. Then I attach magnetic strips to the backs and put them up along the side of my chalkboard. I can move them around on the board to form groups or partners, or to assign tasks. The children enjoy reading their classmates' names. They

also use the heads to complete graphs and sign up for centers during activity time, and they sometimes incorporate them into scenes they draw on the chalkboard.

Chance box

Another system I frequently use is the chance box. In a special box I place large wooden beads, each labeled with a student's name. When it's necessary to choose a child for a job (desirable or not!) or a turn to speak, or to form partnerships or groups, it's easy for me or for the students to draw names. The students recognize this as fair, even though many think their own names are never called: "Are you *sure* it's in there?"

Listening center

I keep sets of read-along books and accompanying tapes in sturdy zip-lock plastic bags. The children know that after listening to a tape they must replace both it and the book carefully so they'll be able to find it again easily. I have a lot of these sets, some with professional tapes and some with tapes we've made ourselves. Some sets have only one book and some have six. At our listening table seven can listen at one time.

Class newsletters

Every day after we've written "The News" together I copy it onto a special newsletter form. It has the school letterhead at the top. By the end of the week the form contains the news of all five days. I may add some notes to the parents (reminders of meetings or other events coming up, requests for new supplies, etc.) before making a copy for each student. Sometimes the students add little drawings to the forms as well. The parents enjoy reading these newsletters with their children. Since we've worked on them together, even beginning readers can read some paragraphs, and the content of the newsletters often reminds them of things they can discuss with their parents. They may have trouble answering the question "What did you do at school today?" but when they read *Our Class News* at home they usually recount interesting things about their school life.

Linda Picciotto's South Park Primary Class Family School

Feb. 2-5

Monday – Today Emily is the scientist. "What is the name of your experiment, Emily?" "It is called The Magic Egg."

Tuesday – We had a good time in the park yesterday afternoon. There was a little ice on the pond. The ducks looked hungry and cold.

Wednesday – Janet brought in her new baby guinea pig. It is white and black and has smooth fur. She named it Rocky Road.

Thursday – We mixed paint yesterday. Yellow and blue make green, red and blue make violet, and yellow and red make orange.

Friday – Today is Buddy Day. We like our buddies. We're going to go to the gym with them. It will be fun!

Don't forget our Family Meeting next Tues. night at Frank's house – 7:30. We'll be making plans for our Winter Carnival and I'll explain the new report card form. Lynda

Interest studies

I use the term "interest studies" rather than "themes" or "units" because of the negative images I connect with those words.

When I think of themes, I think of apples: apple art on the walls, applesauce, trips to the orchards, apple booklets, apple stories, apple poems, apple turkeys (25, all alike!), apple movements in the gym, and math problems printed in apple shapes. There's nothing wrong with these things (except for the identical works of art), but after such total immersion in apples, it's a wonder teacher and students ever want to see the fruit again! Themes like that are artificial. What we're studying doesn't have to permeate the entire classroom. Nor should we choose to study something simply because we have a lot of material about it, or because we've been given a book that has hundreds of activities in all areas of the curriculum centered around that topic.

When I think of units, I think back to my teacher-training days. We were required to assemble units about certain subjects, describe exactly what we would require the students to do and explain how we would evaluate them. The activities were supposed to be interesting and educational, but there was no room for the children's own ideas or input. These units were designed with no particular group in mind; they were to be "laid on" whatever group we were teaching. We all mimeographed extra copies of our units so our fellow teachers would have a store of ready-to-use materials.

So I prefer "interest studies."

Major interest studies

These last for a few weeks or more and are undertaken for a variety of reasons:

◆ We want to set up an all-school study
   (astronomy, Native Peoples, the sea . . .)

◆ I notice that my program is becoming unbalanced
   (I need to add some drama, some experiments with different kinds of graphs, some safety information . . .)

◆ I notice a pronounced student interest in some topic
   (Ryan's interest in turtles is picked up by others in the class, Jerry's science experiment sparks general interest . . .)

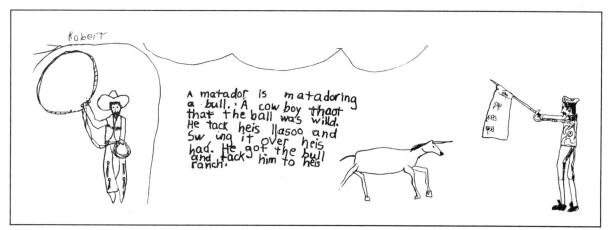

- I know the children will be interested
  (egg incubation, a study of our bodies, learning what animals do in winter . . .
  — these may have been successful with other groups or will, I feel, be particularly
  interesting to this group)
- I want to support a planned field trip
  (a study of salmon before a trip to the river . . .)
- A parent visit sparks class interest
  (a visit from Katie's mother, a nurse, which led to a hospital study; a field trip to
  Eric's mother's university lab, which inspired a snake study . . .)

Minor interest studies

These last from a few hours to a day or two. They might be:

- centered around holidays or celebrations
  (Halloween, Hanukkah, Christmas, Groundhog Day, Valentine's Day . . .)
- part of a long-term study
  (recording weight and height changes during biweekly visits of a new baby,
  measuring the growth of a plant . . .)
- short-term studies launched as a result of a specific interest or event
  (a student question: "Where do bees go in winter?"; a book or film: "Let's learn
  more about sharks"; something a parent or another teacher has brought to our
  attention: "There's a special exhibition at the art gallery your students would
  love"; something that happens in or around the school: a cougar is spotted in the
  park across the street; a field trip or other shared experience: a walk to see Amy's
  father's fishing boat . . .)

I do "lay on" a study if I think it's important, or because it's been successful with
other groups, or when I want to balance my program. The Hannukah study (page 55)
is one example, egg incubation (page 72) another. But those studies never take over
my classroom. I'm careful to maintain those normal daily routines that require the
students to use their own ideas and pursue their own interests.

I'm also careful to share my plans with my fellow teachers so we don't end up
giving our students the same experiences year after year: "How I Spent My Summer
Vacation," "All About Me," "My Family," "Signs of Spring," "Planting Seeds." We talk
together about what we do in our classrooms so we don't repeat too many major
studies. Dinosaurs fascinate children and there are always new facts to be learned
about them, but there are other interesting things in the world as well and it would
be tragic, even for the most devoted dinosaur fans, if they were obliged to study
dinosaurs each year with each new teacher.

Balance is the key word: a balanced program within each classroom, and for each
child a balanced program within his or her school career. I want what I teach to
reflect my students' interests, but I also need to keep an eye on what came before and
what will come after. It's my job not only to nurture my students' interests as they
emerge, but also to inspire new interests by exposing the children to new experiences.

THE PROGRAM AND EVALUATION

A general outline

The following chart outlines the regularly scheduled activities that take place in my classroom and the types of evaluation I use at different times. It also indicates some of the ways parents are involved with the school and the classroom as partners in the education of their children.

DAILY

PROGRAM	EVALUATION	WORKING WITH PARENTS
. Welcome, class gathering, chat . Roll call and more (in French) . Calendar routines (date, day of the week, temperature, weather) . The News . Story . Physical exercise in the classroom . Writing workshop . Reading time . Sharing of writing . Math (throughout the day, with a special time for exploration) . Independent table time (all-day students) . Class meeting (half-day students) . Activity time . Clean-up and other maintenance responsibilities	. Make mental notes about individuals, group dynamics, etc. . Write notes about individuals on cards in my evaluation folder, as opportunities arise . Encourage self-, peer-, and program-evaluation	. Greet them as they bring their children to school . Note parent/child interactions, things to be aware of during the day . Welcome them as assistants, observers and even teachers in some circumstances

TWO OR THREE TIMES A WEEK

PROGRAM	EVALUATION	WORKING WITH PARENTS
. Review the morning or the day . Physical activities (in the gym and/or outside) . Math (focused lessons followed by independent or small-group work) . Music lessons (with the specialist) . Music in the classroom	. Use class lists to: - record student progress in different academic areas - record activities during activity time or on project days - note interactions within groups	. Contact those not seen daily at home, if necessary

WEEKLY

PROGRAM	EVALUATION	WORKING WITH PARENTS
. Writing notebooks . School library visit . Buddy day	. Hold writers' conferences	. Send home class "News of the Week" and the school newsletter

OFTEN THROUGHOUT THE YEAR

PROGRAM	EVALUATION	WORKING WITH PARENTS
. Minor interest studies (see p.18) . Visits to other classrooms for special purposes . Visits from other classes or groups of students . Assemblies (all-school or primary)	. Invite students to add significant work to their portfolios . Start collecting comments I think I'll want to include on the different report cards . Refer students to appropriate specialists, speak with these specialists before and after they've seen the students	. Invite them to: - help in the classroom, assist with special school activities, help with field-trip arrangements, transportation and supervision - attend informal family meetings and all-school general meetings - participate in various school committees - keep in touch through personal contact, notes or phone calls . When necessary, discuss the possibility of involving specialists or establishing special home programs

A FEW TIMES DURING THE YEAR

PROGRAM	EVALUATION	WORKING WITH PARENTS
. Major interest studies (see p.17)	. Collect pre-report data . Carry out special self-evaluation and peer-evaluation activities . Invite students to write their own report cards and (perhaps) assessments of their teacher . Hold special teacher/student conferences . Write report cards . Meet with school-based team to go over class list, identify students who need special help	. Send home the report cards . Invite them to write reports about their own children, or give them to you orally . Arrange student-led conferences and/or hold parent/teacher conferences

ONCE A YEAR

PROGRAM	EVALUATION	WORKING WITH PARENTS
. Special all-school or all-primary events . End-of-year class event . Parent Appreciation Tea . End-of-year trip or activity (families of class members)	. Organize material and files to be sent on with children who are leaving the class . Meet with administrators and fellow teachers to set next year's class composition . Meet with administrators and fellow teachers to discuss programs, major subjects taught this year, plans for next year	. Invite them to help plan and participate in year-end events . Meet with other staff and parent representatives to help set school goals for the following year

A closer look at the outline

Daily

Welcome, class gathering, chat

I greet the children as they come into the classroom, and chat briefly with their parents. When it's time, we gather on the carpet to begin our day together. The roll call, a bit of French, and the update of our calendar are fixed routines my students expect and enjoy, but otherwise our early morning activities vary. Sometimes one of the children has something to share with the class, and sometimes I want to talk about upcoming events, share an exciting new book or announce a new study.

If someone has brought in something to share with the class, we discuss it briefly — or for a longer time if it turns out to be interesting and worthwhile. When Barbara and her mother brought in the family cat, we spent a few minutes admiring it and asking Barbara questions. But since we'd welcomed Carol's cat the week before, we had already pretty well exhausted the subject, so I didn't want to belabor it — and neither did the cat!

I discourage the children from bringing toys. The other students are quickly bored by a parade of furry stuffed animals and plastic muscle men, and such things often cause social problems. Lost teeth and foreign coins don't hold much interest for the group as a whole either. I watch the children carefully during these sharing times, knowing that if their attention wanders something needs to be changed. Sometimes I simply thank a student for bringing in the item and suggest that he or she show it to friends during recess or activity time.

Some children like to speak to the class more than others do. In classes with traditional "show and tell" sessions, those students soon discover that they can talk if they bring something — anything — to class. The result is that the verbal, outgoing children have the floor while the quiet ones listen — or pretend to listen. I've found that by limiting discussion to things of general interest and discouraging a toy parade I can gently encourage the reticent children to join in.

Roll call and more, in French

Roll call is always taken in French. It's easy for the children to answer *"Ici"* or *"Présent(e)"* and to use *"Ça va," "Ça va bien," "Ça va mal."* They are happy to learn a little French if they aren't put on the spot. In the past we've asked students to form sentences far too early, I believe. They need to hear the language first, as they did when they learned their mother tongue.

Sometimes I ask questions, using body language and small drawings on the board to indicate meaning, to which they can simply answer *"Oui"* or *"Non." "Est-ce qu'il fait du soleil?"* I'll ask, drawing a picture of the sun and pointing out the window. *"Non,"* they answer, *"il ne fait pas du soleil."* What do you expect on a Victoria winter day!

Sometimes we tabulate how the students are feeling on a particular day. They are proud when they can understand the French words and, when they are ready, they try to respond more completely to my questions and begin to form some phrases themselves.

On other days I might read a book, discuss what they are wearing or give them commands (*stand up, sit down, turn around, jump*) to carry out. We also sing songs, count the days on the calendar and talk about the days of the week. Everything has a light touch, so French doesn't become a chore. Building good attitudes about other peoples, countries and languages is my main goal.

Calendar routines

Each day a different child has a chance to write the date on a card and add it to our calendar. Another child updates the days-of-the-week chart. A third reads the temperature. Friends are allowed to help. After the temperature reader has written the number on a card, the others guess what it is, and then the number is revealed and the card added to our special temperature calendar. It's a favorite job.

The News

After these routines are finished, we first stretch and then tackle the news of the day. My colleague Margaret Reinhard introduced me to "The News" as a way to teach young children to read and write. This routine lets the children see how words and sentences are put together, and lets them be part of the process.

Usually the subject matter is interesting enough to hold their attention without reminders, but sometimes I need to ask certain children to move, to sit up or to put away distracting objects. I insist on close attention.

I use a portable chalkboard attached to an easel because it's easy for me to use and for the children to reach. First we decide what sentences we want to put on the board for The News that day. Sometimes the discussions are quite lively. Birthdays or a new child joining the class provide immediate subject matter, as do upcoming events the students are excited about, or something that has been discussed earlier. Now and then, when the students are uninspired, I have to prod a bit for items, but not often.

> "Our amaryllis bloomed today. It is beautiful! There are two open flowers and two buds. Another stalk is coming up. The flowers are red."

> "Mary showed us some shells and coral she brought from Hawaii. Some are rough and some are smooth."

> "Today is Eric's birthday. He is turning seven. He brought in cupcakes for us. We'll eat them at recess time. Thanks! Happy birthday!"

Several children might give suggestions about how to phrase the sentences. Sometimes we'll vote on which to use, sometimes I'll choose, and sometimes I'll blend the ideas to make a good sentence that contains elements from two or three different suggestions. Since modeling is so vital, I let them hear me think aloud.

"We could say it that way, but we've already used the word 'we' in the last sentence. Can anyone think of a way to change it around so we don't have to use 'we' again?"

"How about combining Ted's and Carol's suggestions to make this longer sentence: 'We had a great time at the park when we went for a walk yesterday.'"

The children help spell the words as I print them slowly on the board. When I come to an interesting example of how our language works, I quickly explain it to them or ask them about it.

"Why did I put that mark there?" . . . "What kind of letter do we need to use at the beginning of our sentence?" . . . "You have the first and last sounds — now what vowel should go in the middle? 'E'? That would make it say 'pet.' Good guess, Eric. 'A'? That would be 'pat,' but we want 'pit.' 'I'? Right. What other words do you know that end in 'it'? 'Bit . . . sit . . . fit . . .' Now what was the next word we were going to write? Let's read what we have so far."

There is no limit to the kinds of things you can point out while writing The News. Depending on your own interests and the developmental levels of your students, you can include information about word derivation, parts of speech, spelling rules (and exceptions), the formation of the letters themselves ("Everyone practice with your finger in the air"), punctuation and so forth.

I keep a dictionary handy so we can look up the spelling or definition of words I'm not sure about.

"Find the 's' section for me, please, Thomas. I want to check to see if there's an 'e' in 'smokey.'"

The students don't have to raise their hands to answer unless I ask them to. No one is singled out, so everyone feels free to try. Some don't speak out, but they are listening and learning. Sometimes I ask advanced students to wait a few seconds before answering or to spell in their heads so the others have a chance to think.

The children learn different things from this collaborative writing, depending on their readiness. Jamie may be learning the names of the letters and beginning to be aware of the spaces between words. When he hears the words "compound," "vowel" and "apostrophe," they may have no meaning for him at this point. It doesn't matter: he won't be required to complete a worksheet afterwards, and the fact that he's heard the concepts discussed will help him later. Nicky may be learning that it's necessary to drop the 'e' sometimes when adding suffixes, or the concept of root word, or how to form contractions. Both Jamie and Nicky will be able to help with the editing.

"This sentence isn't very interesting. Our readers won't have a picture of what Barbara's cat looks like. What words can we add?"

We use a caret to insert suggestions into the text:

black and white striped
Barbara brought in her ∧ cat this morning. It didn't really like to be at school. It was frightened. Barbara got it at the S.P.C.A.

After we've written as much as I think they can handle that day — usually about three sentences, sometimes all about one subject and sometimes about different things — we read what we've written and edit if necessary. Sometimes we don't edit that day, depending on how long they've been sitting on the carpet and how awake and involved they appear. If they begin to squirm, I increase the tempo or change the focus and soon bring the lesson to a close.

Teachers who have watched this news writing and reading are amazed by the many different phonetic and grammatical concepts we cover in a short period of time — concepts always discussed in context, in ways that are meaningful to the children.

Rereading The News can take many forms. The children love it when I put humor into the reading. Here are some ideas:

◆ I ask volunteers to come to the board to read, following the lines of print with a pointer. They shouldn't point to each separate word, but move the pointer along smoothly as they read, so their eyes aren't focused on individual words. The more able readers usually volunteer first, and that allows the others to follow along and rehearse silently. If a reader is stymied by a word, he or she can ask for help from me or from the class. I usually ask several volunteers to choose one sentence or paragraph each. Not every child will read every day, of course. That would be tedious!

◆ I change the punctuation at the end of an interesting sentence and ask the class to read and reread it, altering their expression to go with the new punctuation mark.

◆ I ask them to read part of the text as if they were robots . . . or Santa Claus . . . or whatever they might suggest. The children whose attention may have wandered are drawn back into the reading by this fun.

◆ I might ask them to read the sentences in their heads as I, or a student, scan them with the pointer.

◆ I play with one of the words.

"What would 'cat' become if I added an 's' in front of the 'c'? . . . or after the 't'? . . . or changed the 'a' to a 'u' and added 'ing'? . . .

◆ I may focus on several words. After the children "take a picture" of how each one is spelled, I erase those words and ask volunteers to come to the board to print them again. The rest of the class helps if necessary. Or I give each child a small chalkboard and let them all try to write the missing words.

"That's almost right, Jerry, but the 'S' in 'share' should be lower case. Can you fix it? . . . Almost, but there has to be a silent letter there. Does anyone remember what it was? . . . Robert, you have the right letters but please help the 'e' and the 'n' change places — they got mixed up. . . . Are all of the words correct now? Yes. A hand for the writers!"

- Ted wants to read the sentence from back to front. Why not? Sometimes the reversed words produce amusing results, and the children watch closely.

- I might erase one of the words and ask the students to choose a different word that would make sense in that position.

  "Today we are going to the *park*. It will be *fun*. Tessa? . . . Today we are going to the *museum*. It will be *interesting*."

- Or I erase several words from the sentences and ask the children to reread The News, remembering which words were erased. Then I erase a few more and have them read, then more, until finally they "read" an empty board. Many skills are involved here, and the children's attention couldn't be better because they're having fun — or perhaps showing off for a visitor.

- Sometimes I decide on a news sentence myself. Instead of writing the words, I draw short lines on the board to stand for each letter, as for a game of Hangman (or Hangletter, as we call it). Then, using the chance box so each child has a turn, I invite them to guess. More advanced students often want to guess whole words, but beginning readers can guess letters — so everyone enjoys the game. As more and more letters or words are filled in, the students become excited and really pay attention, reading and rereading what is on the board, trying to make sense out of it. Finally, a breakthrough! Nicky thinks she knows the whole sentence. Go for it! "Today we are going to look at some works of art." Right!

I leave the news items on the board, and after the students begin their daily writing workshop, I copy them onto the form that will be photocopied and sent home at the end of the week.

Observation

If I want to check the reading progress of individual students, I can call them up to the board while the rest are hard at work. Using one of my evaluation forms, I make notes about how those children read the message we've completed together. I can see if they are moving the pointer from left to right, if they are following the words as they read, or if they have attempted to memorize the text. I can ask them to read individual words or find words I give them. I can help those students who are really reading to practice reading more smoothly, or I can ask them to tell me about certain spelling or punctuation. At the end of each child's assessment I'm careful to point out how much progress he or she is making. They all go back to their tables with satisfied smiles.

Enjoying good books

Critical to the development of my students' interest in reading is listening to, enjoying and discussing good books, articles and poems. The enjoyment of good literature also helps them improve their own writing, builds their personal vocabularies and increases their knowledge of the world. I often read to the class several times during the day. I choose books I know they'll enjoy, aiming for a balance between fiction and nonfiction, but frequently letting the students help in the selection. "Which shall we read, this book about King Edward or the story about penguins in our new magazine? Let's vote." We often read Big Books together, and occasionally chapter books as well. Favorite books brought from home help tie home and school together, and children are always interested in hearing books their friends love.

I often read a book without showing the pictures, reminding the students that the pictures they make in their heads are the best ones. It's fun to compare what each child "saw": "Where was *your* wolf standing? . . . Was he wearing clothes? . . . How big was the dog? . . . What color was the Queen's dress?" Readers need to visualize for good comprehension, and this activity strengthens that ability.

Occasionally I use some type of language arts activity after reading a special book or story. Some stories lend themselves well to a variety of drama experiences, some have plots that are easy to analyze by creating charts or a series of drawings, some present problems that can be debated, and others are perfect for character analysis (see *Literacy through Literature* for examples). Although they can't write summaries as older students often do for a chapter book they're enjoying together or independently, I sometimes ask my younger students to retell stories orally after we've read them together. Follow-up activities like these are very important in helping children develop their reading comprehension — and they add spice to the normal routines of our day. I don't overdo them, however. I want to stress the sheer joy of reading.

Physical activities in the classroom

I usually lead a short exercise session after our morning activities — the children have been sitting on the carpet for quite a while! They often request Simon Says, a game they never seem to tire of. Those who are "caught" help me catch others, so everyone continues to participate. I can incorporate all kinds of activities into this game: stretching, balancing, action songs, in-place aerobic movements, and so forth. Recently I introduced yoga poses as well: "Be a tree . . . be a cobra . . . be a dog . . ." They love to do them and that kind of exercise tends to have a calming effect.

Writing workshop

This process has been described well in other books (see, for instance, *The Learners' Way*). I won't repeat here how children pass through different stages and progress according to their own developmental schedules, but I will say that I've had very good success with this method of teaching writing. The children feel good about their progress and abilities — and themselves.

During writing workshops the students usually write whatever they like. Some stay on one theme for many days, either adding to a story begun earlier or writing yet another piece on a subject that interests them, like cowboys or knights in shining armor, or flowers, rainbows and sunny days. Some talk about events in their own lives. Occasionally I assign a topic. The students who are writing basic simple sentences — "The bunny and the butterfly are friends. They are happy." — often do much more interesting work when they are writing on an assigned topic. If we've all watched a video together, I might ask them to write about one thing they learned. Or I might ask them to write about the walk we took in the park the day before, or about a book we all enjoyed when I read it to them that morning. I often involve them in the decision about what topic to choose. Participating in that kind of decision-making helps them become more imaginative in their own work.

It's not a good idea to push too hard about how much they should write or how "standard" their spelling should be, I've found, although gentle nudges are often productive. Children seem to have their own timetables. If they are exposed to good models and if our expectations are clear, they'll move on when they're ready.

In the meantime, different children need help with their writing at many different levels. That help sometimes takes place informally during the writing period and sometimes during a more formal "writer's conference." I don't like to interfere when the children are writing, and I won't spell for them during this time. At other times during the day I'll scribe or dictate, but not during a writing workshop. I want the students to work independently and feel free to take risks with spelling — not easy for children who are perfectionists by nature or whose parents have stressed the importance of always spelling correctly. Once these children become accustomed to taking risks when they write, their writing becomes much more interesting and they write with more joy. The mechanics of writing become increasingly evident in their work over time, because they are exposed daily to well-written sentences. But the children learn that the important thing about written communication is *meaning*.

In the early stages, the students usually work on their illustrations before they write. Drawing helps them formulate their thoughts and is in itself an excellent intellectual activity that builds many skills. Some need to be reminded about the passage of time, however; they would draw during the entire writing workshop period if given the choice. I allow the children to talk while they are drawing, and even while they are writing, but if their chatting interferes with their work, a reminder and, if necessary, a change in seating may help everyone concentrate better.

When they're finished, the students bring their work to me. I have certain expectations

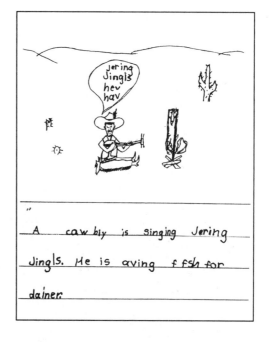

for each student, depending on his or her developmental level, and with these in mind, it takes only a moment to decide if they've completed as much as I think appropriate. If a piece of work is very short and/or hastily printed, I may ask the student to write more, or revise, or proofread. Sometimes I ask the children to read their work to a friend before they bring it to me. After they've read it aloud to me, we talk a little about the drawing and the content of the sentences and, if time permits, have a short, informal writer's conference. If I think I might not be able to decipher the child's writing again later, I make a note on the back of it to remind me what it says. When we've finished, the children file their writing in the "Author's Circle" folder or in their own writing folders, depending on the plan for the day.

Observation

The following examples, written by children in my class of five- and six-year-olds one morning in the fall, illustrate the wide range of abilities found in any classroom. In spite of the differences, however, each child felt successful!

"Ths A Tre."

This is a tree.

"Ther is A MOtan it is KOLroFAL tHe SAN IS HINiNG i LiK it."

There is a mountain. It is colorful. The sun is shining. It like it.

"SAr is A Bot Hos HArS AAre NABALING At tHe BotHos"

There is a boathouse. Sharks are nibbling at the boathouse.

"Hr is a canoo. the canoo is tid on a roc. Ther are weds stumping."

Here is a canoe. The canoe is tied on a rock. There are weeds thumping.

"This is a story: Salmon like it in the strems. They have lots of fun, but thay go one by one. Salmon think it's fun, one by one. Salmon think it's fun."

(Nicky often wrote poems and stories during writing workshop.)

Writings like these are windows into my students' thought processes. Reading them helps me to recognize the needs of each child and to know what concepts to emphasize during our news writing. I soon learn which children need extra help to notice patterns or to understand how our language works.

Reading time

My students know it's reading time after recess. As soon as they come in they each choose a book or two from the large supply in our room and find a private spot where they can read independently. I provide some guidance, if necessary, concerning appropriate books and behavior. Of course I read during this time as well, at least for part of the period, to set the tone and provide a model — and because I enjoy reading. After 10-15 minutes I announce that they can share their book with a friend or move to the tape center. Then I circulate, listen to the students read, and make mental or written observations.

For variety, I sometimes put out on the tables several sets of multiple copies of easy, familiar books and ask the students to form groups to read one or two stories with their friends. These are inevitably mixed-ability groups, and there's usually one student in each group who becomes the leader as they all work together to read the stories of their choice. Sometimes I'll have these groups read with me, usually in unison, while I make mental notes of their progress.

On some days, at the end of the reading period, we share the books we've been reading. Some children might read or paraphrase a favorite page or two, or show their favorite illustration, while others just tell their classmates what they've been reading. They often like to know a little about my book or article as well. If some children have been reading together, they may decide to share their book by reading the story in unison. During unison reading, even non-readers feel that they're participating as they follow along a split second behind their reading peers.

We may begin or end reading time by reading together an enlarged book or a poem on a chart.

Sharing of writing

After reading time we often hold a formal Author's Circle. Some or all of the students read their day's writing to their classmates, who ask questions about the content and make comments about the writer's progress. Modeling is very important here to make sure that all comments are positive and helpful. All students need to feel comfortable about sharing their work, no matter what their level of competence is, knowing that they will be supported in their efforts by their friends and teacher.

Observation

"I really like the way you drew that dinosaur, Carl. I especially like the teeth. Is it a Tyrannosaurus Rex?"

"You used spaces between your words today, and I see some words in standard spelling."

"I like your rainbow, Sarah. You used lots of lower case letters and separated your words!"

"I like the colors you used for the sky."

"I thought you were going to finish the story you started yesterday, Michael. I wanted to know how it ended. Your story today it different!"

In Author's Circle they practice the important skills of self- and peer-evaluation. They learn the vocabulary and the observational and analytical skills that will help them explain their progress to their parents during student-led conferences. This is one way of helping children assess and take responsibility for their own progress and achievements instead of making them dependent on the judgments of adults.

If there's another adult in the classroom, I usually divide the children into two or more groups to allow more thorough discussion of each child's work than is possible in a larger group.

Math time

Most days we have a math activity time. I ask the children to choose materials or games from our well-supplied cupboards to use on their own or with a partner. I take advantage of these periods to evaluate individual students and make notes on my individual or class-list forms. Often we meet afterwards to discuss what they worked with and what they discovered. To help them become more aware of their learning and to introduce them to the vocabulary of mathematics, I sometimes ask them to raise their hands if they were counting . . . working with patterns . . . computing . . . graphing . . . planning . . . solving a problem . . . estimating . . . weighing . . . The students are sometimes surprised to find they've been doing many of these things as they worked.

Independent table time

After lunch my half-day (kindergarten) students arrive. I like to spend about 20 minutes with them on the carpet, for a chat and perhaps a quick calendar discussion, news writing, a read-aloud or a math activity. My all-day students know they are expected to work almost silently at the tables during this time, reading, writing or drawing. They look forward to this quiet time of the day. Those who can't work quietly are invited to join us on the carpet.

Activity time

Activity time is a very important part of the program, and the students feel really cheated if I have to cancel it for some reason or another. During this period they are allowed to select their own activities. If too many choose a center that can't accommodate them all at one time, we make sign-up lists on the board and use a timer to signal group changes.

I put new materials out often, and frequently reintroduce old-but-forgotten games or supplies I think they might enjoy again. Usually they already have ideas about what they want to do. Many construct things using items from the art box, which is constantly being added to by both me and the parents, and from the paper supply cupboard. Others make their own booklets, read books, engage in dramatic play in the playhouse, or use the math materials in a variety of ways. Still others share the Playmobil sets, the blocks, the water table, the playdough, the Plasticine, the computers or the paints. Often someone organizes a puppet show or a play.

This is my time to watch the children and record which ones have worked together and what things they have chosen to do. The creativity they display during these periods is remarkable. Sometimes they have enough time after clean-up to show each other what they've made.

Two or three times a week

Review of the morning or the day

It's no wonder children can't answer their parents' question, "What did you do at school today?" During a review of the morning at 11:50, children this young have a hard time remembering what they did — and in what order — just that morning! With practice they get better, however. The exercise benefits them in many ways. As well as improving their memories and giving them practice with sequencing, it helps them to become more aware of their own learning: "Look how much we do at school!"

Physical activities outside the classroom

The children love to go to the gym and play on the playground. They participate in a variety of activities, some teacher-directed (warm-ups, exercises, play with the parachute, a new game, a new dance), some student-chosen ("What game shall we play? . . . What game do you know that you want to teach the others?"), and some free activities using a variety of available equipment. If an activity doesn't work well, or if a child has been injured, we stop to talk about it. Usually the students have very good ideas about how we can change the rules to make a game safer or more fun.

Math lesson

Although I like to teach much of our math throughout the day as "teachable moments" present themselves and as part of our interest studies, I often teach specific lessons during our daily math time, to ensure that I'm covering all areas of the math curriculum. We enjoy working together with numbers and mathematical concepts, using manipulative materials. Individual chalkboards are useful as well. Sometimes I introduce a concept and then give the students a problem to solve, encouraging them to use the materials as they work out their solutions. They can help each other, but I don't let them call out the answers when they solve the problem, since I want to give the slower workers time to think for themselves. When they've all indicated that they have an answer, I let everyone answer at once or ask for a volunteer. Then I ask several different children to tell us how they were thinking while they were working. It's always interesting to see how many different ways there are to look at even quite simple problems. I'm careful not to embarrass anyone, since I want the students to feel free to take risks. I also give them opportunities to suggest problems for their classmates to solve.

Music

We're lucky to have an excellent music teacher. Marne's always positive and encouraging, but she's demanding as well, so the students are making good progress in their singing and in their knowledge about music. We also sing and play musical games in the classroom several times a week. These sing-along sessions provide a nice balance to the more formal music lessons.

Weekly

Writing notebook

Once a week, usually on Wednesday morning (because my half-day students are present), I ask the students to complete their writing workshop in their personal notebooks instead of on the usual loose pieces of paper. This gives me a cumulative record of their writing and artwork that's very useful when I write report cards and conference with parents. The students who have been in my class for two or three years also like to go back to see how they used to write and draw "when we were little."

Library

We go to the library together once a week to exchange books and enjoy a story read by our librarian. We also use the library informally at other times during the week, and the librarian helps us collect materials for our interest studies.

Writer's conference

I try to have a formal writer's conference with every all-day student at least once a week, in addition to the shorter, informal conferences that occur daily. I keep a record to make sure I don't miss anyone. During this formal conference the student and I read and discuss a completed piece of writing. We discuss the content first and then analyze the writing.

I write the piece out "in standard spelling" while the child watches, and we compare it with the original. We note how many letters were correct or "good guesses." Often the students can tell me what other letters they could have included, where they should have put periods or other punctuation, which letters are upper case that should be lower case, and which letters could be more neatly drawn: the specifics depend on the child's developmental level.

At the end of the conference we decide what things the student will work on next.

Carl will try to write longer sentences using more describing words.

Sarah will try to remember to use periods at the ends of her sentences and to form her 'n's more carefully so they won't look like 'h's.

Jerry will work more slowly so his paper will look neater, and he'll remember to spell the word 'they' with an 'e' instead of an 'a.'

Kate will read her sentences out loud quietly, and add missing letters and punctuation.

Thomas is ready to start using some letters of the alphabet to stand for his sentences instead of the "pretend" writing he's been using.

Tessa will think of more interesting ways to begin her sentences — no more "This is . . ."

Janet will spend less time on her drawing so she can write more.

After a few of these conferences, the students are often able to decide on their own what they could be doing to improve their writing.

Buddy day

Once a week we meet with our "buddies" from a class of older students. The buddy pairs engage in activities the other teacher and I design to help them get to know each other and to provide them with a variety of educational experiences. I take time to discuss the sessions with the students, sometimes while the older and younger students are together, but more often after the older students have gone. I need feedback about their relationships with their buddies. Often they have very good suggestions for each other when someone brings up a problem such as: "My buddy keeps talking to his friends instead of to me." I listen to their reactions to the activities, solicit ideas for future meetings, and help make sure that the buddy days run smoothly so they provide positive experiences for everyone. Some examples of buddy activities might be:

♦ Share books together.

♦ Make a class Big Book together, with each pair working on a page to create the text and illustration.

Observation

Once we asked them to divide their papers in half and to follow this pattern: "Sarah feels little when she _____. Sarah feels big when she_____." To set the stage, I read the book *Big or Little* by Kathy Stinson. Two pairs came up with the following text:

"Ryan feels big when he rides his new bike. Ryan feels little when his mother makes him wear funny hats."

"Jamie feels big when he can tie his own shoe. Jamie feels little when he can't reach the cupboard."

♦ Collaborate on an art project: paint giant flowers that we'll use to decorate the gym for the spring assembly, draw the daffodils Mary brought in . . .

♦ Write Valentine poems together, with the older buddies doing the writing.

♦ Exchange gifts they've made for each other.

♦ Go for a walk in the park to look for signs of spring, sketch, or feed the ducks.

♦ Learn a new folk dance together in the gym.

Buddy time helps the two groups of children see each other as individuals and not just as "big kids" and "little kids" on the playground. My young students are thrilled to see and speak to their big buddies at recess, and their big buddies often look out for them and help when they have injuries or hurt feelings.

Often throughout the year

Portfolios

I've initiated a system of portfolios in my classroom. Each student has a legal-size file folder that fits in a special box, and in these they put work that either they or I think is of special importance. Some pieces might illustrate new abilities or be especially interesting in content. They might include pieces of art the students are proud of, or a math graph they completed on their own. Everything put into the file is dated, and the reason for its inclusion is written on a simple form that's glued onto the back. We use a different form for a new accomplishment that can't be placed in the file — a new physical or social skill, for example: "I learned how to swim the length of the pool" . . . "I can go clear across on the rings" . . . "I made my first basket in gym." (See pages 8-9 of *Evaluation: A Team Effort*.)

Things can be put into the file any time during the year, and periodically I ask the students to go through their recent writing samples and choose their best work. On the forms I write the students' exact words.

Observation

When the students can tell me precisely why they have chosen a piece of work for their portfolio, I know they are becoming aware of their own learning.

"I worked hard on this and I really like the picture."

"I used spaces for the first time."

"I used lots of standard words."

"My picture has a lot of action in it."

Assemblies

Our school has a variety of assemblies throughout the year: the universal "school rules reminder" type, performances by groups of various kinds, class-organized celebrations of holidays to which other classes or individuals can contribute, and awards assemblies. Bimonthly we hold a student-organized assembly during which individual students or small groups perform on musical instruments, sing, recite poems, present short plays or even tell jokes. Senior students organize the presentations, set up the sound system and act as announcers. These assemblies provide wonderful experience for the participants, and everyone enjoys them.

In our school, student service and participation are acknowledged publicly. All older students volunteer to do some kind of school service, and we think it's important to acknowledge the service they give as safety patrol members, library monitors, lunch monitors, office helpers and members of sports teams. As they watch awards being accepted at the awards assemblies, the younger students begin to think about how they might want to serve the school community when they are older.

At the end of the year all primary students are called up individually to receive a beautiful certificate stating that they have completed the year in a particular class. We don't believe in choosing the top students in different academic or citizenship categories. It's our belief that most students *want* to succeed. Those who have difficulty concentrating or complying with our requests often have emotional or family problems that interfere with their schooling. Advanced students don't have to be told they are performing well in their classes — they know. They are doing well because they are capable and because they are motivated and interested, not because they might receive an award for their efforts.

A WHOLE YEAR OF LEARNING TOGETHER

My plan for the year

Before school began in September, I had an outline of the year in mind. I knew the basic daily and weekly schedule I was going to follow. I knew some of the events that were planned for the entire school. I had selected some of the major and minor interest studies I was going to explore with the children. My outline also left a lot of room for new ideas — the children's, mine and those I would collect during the course of the year from parents, fellow teachers, books and magazines. I'd have ample opportunity to take advantage of the unexpected experiences the class and I were sure to share.

The chart below contains the "bare bones" outline of minor and major interest studies and special events I began the year with. You'll see from the descriptions that follow that some of my plans materialized, some were abandoned or modified, and many new studies emerged as we all worked and learned together.

SEPTEMBER

- Begin *minor year-long interest study:* safety — home, school, street
- Begin *minor year-long interest study:* Thomas's new baby sister Kyla — child development
- Begin *minor year-long interest study:* biweekly cooking — assemble cookbooks

OCTOBER

- *Minor interest study:* Thanksgiving
- *Minor interest study:* Halloween — trip to pumpkin patch, possible bat or spider study
- *Minor interest study:* art gallery — possible visit

NOVEMBER

- *Major interest study:* salmon

DECEMBER

- *Minor interest study:* amaryllis bulb — growth graph

- *Minor interest study:* Hanukkah
- *Class event:* winter concert presentation
- *School event:* primary ice-skating party
- *Class event:* potluck family dinner

JANUARY

- *Trip:* police station — for safety study

FEBRUARY

- *Minor interest study:* Chinese New Year, including lunch at a Chinese restaurant
- *Minor interest study:* Valentine's Day

MARCH

- *Trip:* Tom Thumb Safety Village, for safety study — follow-up mapping activities

APRIL

- *Minor interest study:* egg incubation

- *Trip:* public library — tour, get library cards

MAY

- *Minor interest study:* Mother's Day — gift or card?
- *Trip:* Swan Lake Nature Centre, if possible

JUNE

- *Minor interest study:* Father's Day
- *Minor interest study:* Parent Appreciation Tea
- *Minor interest study:* "class annual"
- *School event:* Games Day
- *Class event:* family trip (camping? day outing?)
- *School event:* primary classes' beach trip

How the year unfolded

Safety: A minor interest study becomes major

At our first staff meeting in September the school nurse told us she was interested in holding a Health and Safety Fair in the spring. She asked the staff if we would be interested in contributing to the event, and everyone agreed it was a good idea. Each teacher decided on an area of responsibility for his or her class. Marg (the other early-primary teacher) and I decided we'd focus on safety in the streets.

Right away I began to involve my students in studies about safety, using an excellent source produced by our provincial insurance company. The students were given "passports" to fill with colorful stickers they could earn by participating in lessons and activities relating to specific safety subjects. They loved collecting the stickers.

September

The children have to cross a busy street to reach our playground. I asked our grade-seven lunch monitors, Nathanda and Chrissy, who served as crossing guards from time to time, to prepare a lesson and demonstration about crossing streets safely. They were pleased to do so.

I invited them to meet us outside before recess, dressed in their reflective vests and hats and carrying their STOP flags. My students marched back and forth across the street, taking turns pretending to be crossing guards, while Nathanda and Chrissy supervised them. To early-primary children, the youngest in the school, crossing guards seem very mature and wise . . . and lucky! They loved having a chance to be one for a few moments!

September

Across from our school is a very large city park that's patrolled, from June through September, by a police officer on horseback. I phoned the police station to make an appointment for a school visit, and we met the officer and her horse on the playground. The students had many questions to ask:

- What do you do in the park?
- How do you catch bad guys?
- How old is your horse?
- Does he belong to you?
- What does he eat?
- Can we pet him?
- Where does he sleep at night?
- Does he like being a police horse?
- Can we see your gun?

Back in the classroom we discussed the visit and listed the things we had learned. Then I gave the students the choice of writing to the constable or drawing pictures to send to her. Some chose to write *and* draw. I suggested that they might want to work in pairs, or even in larger groups.

October

A young man from our Regional Safety District came in with a bicycle and related safety equipment. He showed a film and led a discussion about bicycle safety. If *he* thought it was smart — even "cool" — to wear a helmet and a reflective jacket and to stop at stop signs, maybe they should too. They certainly listened to him more closely than they would have to their nice but even-older-than-their-parents teacher! We promised in our class thank-you letter to be safe on our bicycles.

October

Our substitute lunch monitor, Julie, had been having some trouble at home and had been creating problems for herself and others in her classroom. She was a competent, kind helper in my room and I thought she might like another opportunity to be of assistance, so I asked her if she'd bring her bicycle into our room after recess. She appeared promptly without a reminder.

My students gathered around Julie and her bicycle and told her the names of some of the parts of the bike. They also told her what they remembered from the safety talk earlier in the week. Julie was impressed. She added a few things they hadn't mentioned and told them how she used a light in the evening and always wore a helmet.

Then I passed out small drawing boards with several sheets of paper and a piece of charcoal for each student, and they all found comfortable places to sit. I told them they could draw a whole bicycle or just a wheel, the handlebars, the light, a pedal — whatever they found interesting. They could spend a long time on one picture or they could complete a series of quick sketches. They settled down quickly and produced wonderful sketches that I later displayed on our bulletin boards. Julie and I drew too.

This turned out to be one of those classroom times when everything seems just right: everyone was content, relaxed and involved.

November

When Sonja's mother Carole was helping in my room I pressed her into service in the role of an elderly pedestrian who was somewhat unsteady on her feet. She walked one way along the sidewalk while we walked towards her. I told my students to forget their manners and walk ahead in pairs as if she weren't there. They did, and soon one of them bumped into Carole. She gave a little shriek, wobbled for a few seconds and then fell over on the grass. The children were startled and silent, and I became concerned: she had been so convincing that I thought she might really be injured.

After we'd determined that our "fallen elderly neighbor" was all right, I asked her a few questions:

"How did you feel when you saw the children coming towards you?" . . . "Frightened. I've already broken one hip and I'm so afraid of falling again."

"What should we do the next time?" . . . "If everyone would just move over to give me a place on one side of the sidewalk I'd be very happy. I can't walk well on the grass."

"Is there anything else we should do?" . . . "Smile and say hello. I like children but they make me nervous when they move quickly."

The children agreed that many of our local residents must feel that way. They remembered the people at the rest home we visited at Halloween (see page 47), many of whom could hardly walk.

We settled on a signal: I would raise my right hand when they should move to the right side of the sidewalk. First we all had to agree which was the "right side." Next we practiced. This time as Carole approached us I gave the signal and all of the students moved over. Many said "Good morning" or "Hello" to her as she tottered past. Back in the classroom I distributed the Sidewalk Safety stickers for their passports.

January

I arranged a tour of the city police station. The children were most impressed with the jail cells, with the woman who answered the 911 calls, with the huge motorcycles parked in the back, and with the big books of mug shots in the fingerprinting room. The children were fingerprinted if they wished, and were given their prints to take home. Some refused. Maybe they didn't want to get ink on their fingers, or perhaps they thought it meant they had done something wrong.

February

We had already discussed the importance of seatbelts. I asked the students if they'd like to complete a survey of how many drivers really use them. Of course they agreed. I divided them into four groups in preparation for a walk to the local four-way-stop corner. They each took a clipboard for keeping track, in whatever way they wanted, of the number of drivers who were wearing seatbelts. At the end of our survey they should be able to tell their classmates:

- How many cars stopped at their corner.
- How many drivers were wearing seatbelts.
- How many drivers were not wearing seatbelts.

In the past I had set up tally systems for them. However, I found that many of my young students were confused and frustrated by systems I had thought would be easy to understand. Setting up their own systems worked much better and was more meaningful to them. Many used a system like the one I would have suggested, for we often tally things on the board together in class. Sometimes they had trouble reading their own figures at the end, but it didn't really matter. At this stage it was the process that counted.

They had a good time watching the traffic at the corner. Michael remarked that he felt important, like a scientist, when he was taking his notes. Mary spent much of her energy — predictably, I know her — seeing how many drivers would wave at her. Ted was more interested in the vehicles themselves, particularly the trucks.

Back in the classroom I asked each group to meet to prepare a report of its findings. I heard interesting conversations as I walked about taking notes and asking questions I thought might help them with their reports.

After 20 minutes we met to share the reports. Some groups gave precise numbers and used the large chalkboard to list the "yes" and "no" numbers. Others, whose members had been distracted by other interests or whose systems had proved hopelessly confusing, were able to make more general statements: "There were more drivers who used seat belts and fewer who didn't." Armando and Sarah, two strong-willed leaders, had been in the same group. Since they couldn't agree on the numbers and neither was willing to bend, they solved the problem by giving two different reports. The other members of the group simply chose which report they'd support. This was a good solution, I thought, one that left everyone happy.

Observation

Janet, one of those children who has difficulty deciding what to write during writing workshop and who was having trouble moving beyond "This is a bunny. He is happy," wrote this about the experience: "Toda we lrnd abt trafk sfte. Sm ov the clas wer on govrnmnt strt and sm ov the clas wer on mishigun strt."

Kate wrote: "I lerned that som peple put on setbels. I lerned a lot. Use your setbels. Stop at stopsins. I saw 19 peple whring there setbels."

Nicky: "Today we did servays. I got mostly drivrs waring seetbelts. I didn't get eny drivrs not waring seetbelts. It was very fun. I was on the west cornr."

Ellen: "When we watchd for trafek I fawnd out that moost peple aer carfuol daving. Som peple aer't carfuol. Most peple whr setblts."

March

Creating safety posters was one way to earn the art sticker in the Passport program. I thought we could also use these as our contribution to the Health and Safety Fair.

I asked the students to think of all of the safety rules we had learned this year. It was a challenge to come up with 25, but they did it! I recorded them on the board using symbols and short words that everyone could read or remember. Then I asked each child to think about which ones they would like to choose.

The chance box determined the order in which the children could come to the board to claim a safety rule by initialing it. As soon as they signed up, they began their work. My only instruction was that their drawings had to be large — people had to be able to see them from across the room. I suggested also that they be colorful.

Don't drink and drive.

Observation

Christopher was really upset because his name was called near the last and all four of his favorites had been spoken for. The remaining rules were *boring*. I told him I was sure he could think of a solution. He pouted for a while behind the bookcase, but when he came back he told me, "I thought of a new rule that we forgot." It turned out to be very much like the one he had really wanted, but he had changed the words a bit to make it a little different: DON'T DRIVE DRUNK instead of DON'T DRINK AND DRIVE, which had been Michael's pick.

Polly drew a happy little girl with a purple dress and stick arms sitting in a car seat with a bold black line across her body. Her caption, which I printed at the bottom of the poster for her, was FASTEN YOUR SEAT BELT.

Jerry drew a large round-faced person with arrows around his head going up, down, left and right. The caption: LOOK FORWARDS, BACKWARDS, LEFT AND RIGHT BEFORE YOU CROSS.

Janet's was inspired by an earlier safety lesson. She drew a line of students on a sidewalk walking towards an old lady: LOOK OUT ON THE SIDEWALK — DON'T RUN INTO PEOPLE!

Thomas loves to draw scenes with lots of action. He specializes in things blowing up. He had picked a good safety rule for his poster: WHEN YOU DRIVE, STAY ON YOUR OWN SIDE OF THE ROAD. He drew the accident that happened when a driver hadn't followed the rule. Very colorful!

April

Our trip to the Tom Thumb Safety Village was every bit as successful as I knew it would be. Over the years it has often been listed by my students as the favorite field trip of the year. The Village is a miniature town layout, complete with roads, sidewalks, real traffic lights, a gas station and railroad crossings.

```
Sarah

        I liked Tom Thumb Safety Village.  I was in
     a purple car.  I followed the rules.  I did not
     make any mistakes.  It was very good.
```

The children listened carefully to the instructor. Then half of them drove around the little town in colorful pedal cars while the rest practiced being pedestrians. They changed roles after awhile. Both groups had to obey all of the traffic rules. Our teacher at the Village was strict: speeders and jay-walkers were lectured.

Back at school, I broke my rule about never giving students patterns for art, and asked Marg, who teaches across the hall, to show my class how to make little house-shaped boxes out of squares of paper. Together the children built a small safety village in our classroom sandbox. Many things were added to the town: mountains, railroads, trees, people, farms, cars and road signs, some hand-made and some borrowed from our classroom play sets.

After we had worked together on the class town, I asked the students to form groups to construct their own villages on large pieces of tagboard. Most worked in pairs or groups of three, but a few chose to work independently. Some children worked a long time on these projects and demonstrated many creative ideas.

I assessed the students' work habits and social skills while they worked on these little towns. When all were finished, they shared their projects with their classmates, so I could make notes about their speaking skills as well.

To determine which group members could take the finished villages home, the students decided we should use the "pick a number" method. The child in each group whose number was closest to the one I wrote down in secret would be the winner for that group.

April

Our all-school Health and Safety Fair was held in the gym. My students participated in a number of events organized by the different classes. They learned how to make a sling for a broken arm in one corner of the gym, practiced escaping from a burning building in another, and learned how to wash their hands properly under the supervision of still another group of older students. They took their favorite stuffed animals through a health check-up set up by the school nurse. Our own beautiful safety posters decorated the walls.

May

I read that the provincial insurance company was offering $500 awards to the classes or schools submitting the best traffic safety projects. As we had already studied many aspects of safety, it seemed like a good idea to apply for this award. We would have to write letters and organize our submission.

We thought of all the things we had done during the year. Pairs of students volunteered to be responsible for the write-up of each activity. I proofread their contributions with them and then printed their descriptions in an enlarged book. Illustrations and even some photographs were included on appropriate pages. The class helped me write an introduction and a table of contents. We also submitted a bound collection of the safety posters from the Health and Safety Fair.

One day we received a letter notifying us of our success! A few weeks later a representative came to our classroom to present the award. We invited our principal to attend the ceremony. After a discussion and vote, we bought a new Playmobil set (the zoo) with the prize money. There was enough left over for some new games, books and math materials as well.

Summary

This safety study gave me the opportunity to involve the children in a great variety of activities that touched on almost all areas of the curriculum. They used art when they completed their posters and when they drew the bicycle. For reading practice, I had assembled small booklets with one safety rule on each page; the students illustrated them and took them home to read with their parents. They learned a lot in the area of social studies when we made community visits and discussed the importance of respecting the rules and the rights of others. They needed to use their math skills in real ways when they worked on their safety villages and when they did their traffic surveys. A truly relevant and cross-curricular interest study!

Tadpoles: A new minor interest study emerges

In September Ted, a new half-day student, and his mother Rachel brought in two tadpoles in a tub. They were the largest tadpoles we had ever seen and the students were very interested in them. I asked Rachel to take a small group to the library to borrow all of the books they could find about frogs. The rest of us took turns examining the tadpoles closely.

"Look! One of them has back legs!" . . . "There are stripes on the tails." . . . "They look like they're wearing black lipstick." . . . "Think they can see us?" . . . "Can we keep them?"

We spread the books out on the carpet and looked through them until someone found a photograph of tadpoles that looked like ours. They turned out to be young bullfrogs.

Ted decided to leave the tadpoles at school. He and his mother said they would feed them and bring in fresh pond water from time to time so they would stay healthy.

Rachel also called the museum to arrange for a frog expert to come to the class. He brought tadpoles like ours at different stages of development so we could see how ours were going to look. He told us it would take three more years for them to become mature frogs. He also brought newts, salamanders and splay-footed frogs.

The little splay-footed frogs became our favorites. They had buried themselves in the dirt in his terrarium, but he unearthed them and placed them on top of the soil. We watched as they used their big flat feet in such a way that their bodies moved quickly straight down under the dirt: feet first, eyes last! To thank him we produced a "coffee table book" as a gift: each child drew a colorful picture featuring his or her favorite amphibian. I scribed the dictated sentences on the appropriate pages.

The class's interest in frogs continued after the visit, so I showed a video from the media center and read aloud a few more books some class members had brought in. I also searched through *Ranger Rick* magazines to find good articles and photographs. We read Arnold Lobel's *Frog and Toad* series with new interest, and one small group of students presented one of the tales as a play. The librarian helped by providing us with other traditional tales and modern stories that feature frogs in main-character roles. It was fun to compare them. Why is it that princes are always turned into frogs?

Frogs continued to show up in the writing and drawing of many of the students during the following weeks. Ted made a book entitled "From Tadpole to Frog." An older student helped him with the words, but he completed the delightful drawings himself. He decided to take it home instead of adding it to our classroom collection.

Ultimately this was only a minor interest study in length for most students, but for some it provided a year-long focus.

Kyla: A year-long minor interest study begins

Thomas's mom Anna had a baby girl during the summer. I decided that it would be fun for us to watch her grow during her first year.

I prepared a "Big Book of Kyla's First Year" with blank pages for recording her height, weight, physical changes, speech development, sleeping patterns and diet. Anna planned to bring Kyla to school every two weeks, and the children would help me complete the pages after each visit. What an opportunity for writing with a purpose! I knew they'd like to illustrate the pages and sketch Kyla from time to time. The book would make a nice gift for Anna at the end of the year.

The first visit had everybody excited, especially Thomas, who was happy to share his little sister with us. I set up the weighing and measuring station and we took our first notes.

Kyla's first year

Age:	8 weeks
Weight:	7 kg
Height:	67 cm
Physical changes:	Smiles a lot now, seems to recognize voices and faces; sometimes will follow a moving object with her eyes.
Speech:	Makes cooing noises.
Sleep patterns:	Sleeps a little longer at night but still wakes several times for feeding.
Diet:	Still breast milk, but tried some rice cereal and banana flakes.

(Thomas: "Yeah, and she was really surprised. She made a funny face and spit it all out. She looked like this." He demonstrated, to everyone's amusement.)

We really enjoyed the biweekly experiences of weighing, measuring, watching and asking about the baby. Anna and Thomas did a wonderful job explaining and demonstrating her development. Once Anna gave Kyla a bath in the classroom. The children cheered Kyla on when she showed us how she could crawl and again, later in the year, when she took her first unsteady steps. Thomas carried her around so everyone could have a good look at the little serrated top of her first tooth when it appeared.

However, when it came time to do our write-ups I found that most of the students were uninspired. Some helped with the sentence construction and writing, but I noted widespread inattention and restlessness. So I gave up the idea of the student-written book. Instead, I filled in the information myself. We still referred to it to find out things like how much she'd weighed two weeks before, so we could compute how many grams she'd gained.

I was sorry to abandon the book — it seemed like such a good idea. Maybe the students were bored because they were already doing enough writing during the day. Maybe writing up the notes required more attention span that they'd developed yet. Maybe they couldn't really see a purpose for the book. In any event, I was reminded of an important rule in teaching: watch the kids and take your lead from them. So we kept on with the visits but forgot the language-experience part of the study.

I sent questionnaires home so the students could record how old they were when they got their first tooth, sat up alone, started walking and said their first word. They had a good time interviewing their parents, and the facts brought back provided us with several graphing opportunities.

Observation

Carl had his first tooth when he was four months old, Sonja had one at six months, and Eric was toothless for almost a year! We noted that Tessa was walking at eight months, Ted took his first steps around 12 months, but Sarah hadn't even begun to stand alone until she was a year and a half!

"But can you all walk now?" I asked. Of course! "Do you all have teeth?" Yes — and some had begun to get their second set! So this was a good lesson: "You'll all be independent readers one day, and you'll all be accomplished writers. You'll all understand numbers. You'll all be able to ride bicycles. Different people learn things at different times. You mustn't be discouraged if you can't read as well as your friend or write as well as your brother, or if you still need training wheels. You will learn in your own good time."

When Morgan joined our class at the beginning of October, Moira, her mother, was due to have a baby at any time. I talked to Moira and found that she was willing to come in sometime when Cynthia, a parent who is an obstetrician, could visit our class. Using wonderful books to illustrate her talk, Cynthia told the children "everything they ever wanted to know" about childbirth. Moira lay down on our couch and wow, was she big! Cynthia measured Moira and listened to the baby's heartbeat, and showed us how the baby was positioned. We could see it move! Morgan sat near her mother and helped with the explanations.

It was fun to greet Sam, Morgan's new brother, when he was old enough to come to the school, but I didn't try to repeat the child development experience we'd enjoyed with Kyla. I knew interest wouldn't be high. It was time to move on to something else.

Cooking: Another year-long minor interest study begins

One sure road to student interest is through their stomachs! I've used my "cooking days" system for several years and I've always found it successful.

Two parents volunteer to be in charge of cooking days, usually held twice a month, working with me to set up a wide range of cooking and food preparation experiences. Food and the necessary equipment are sent in by different parents each time, and the volunteers make sure that at least one other adult will be in the classroom to help out on the big day. I'm in charge of the logistics, the teaching and general crowd control. Depending on the recipe of the day, the students may be working in small groups or individually.

One day I read *Stone Soup*. We washed a small rock, put it into a cooking pot and filled the pot with water. Then different groups of children peeled, cut and added a variety of vegetables and spices to the mixture. We went for a walk in the park while the soup simmered. ("Just like the Three Bears," somone said.) Back in the classroom, the group in charge ladled the soup into cups and served it with crackers. It was delicious.

At Halloween we made "pumpkin faces." The children arranged themselves around our five round tables where my helpers had arranged supplies for creating faces on rice cakes. We used peanut butter and cream cheese for the "glue" and raisins, carrot rounds, shredded coconut and pumpkin seeds for the hair and features. Before eating, we all walked around the tables to see and admire the many different creations.

When we baked bread, each of five groups had a specific task: (1) mix the yeast, water and sugar; (2) add the flour and mix; (3) knead and leave to rise; (4) form into loaves; (5) bake, cut and serve. This time the cooking was done in the staff room instead of the classroom because the parents involved thought it would be easier to manage.

After enjoying the food that's prepared, the students gather on the carpet to help me write the recipe on the board. Many skills are involved in putting the steps in order and deciding how to write each instruction. When we've finished, we reread what we've written to make sure it's correct and complete enough to satisfy them. We always start out with "Wash your hands" and end with "Enjoy it!" Even non-readers can read those lines!

I copy the recipe onto the bottom half of a piece of notebook paper, photocopy a class set and three-hole punch them. The next day I distribute these papers, we read our recipe again, and then the children add illustrations. Afterwards, they put their pages into the sorter so they'll remember to take them home. If I think their families

might want to make the recipe at home, I photocopy the more detailed conventional recipe on the back. Each student keeps a three-hole recipe book at home and adds new recipes all year. Their drawings of the food or its preparation are wonderful, and these recipe books often become cherished souvenirs.

After they've had these recipe experiences, many of the students use the same format when writing up their science experiments.

Pumpkin Faces

1. Wash your hands.
2. Put a rice cake on a paper towel.
3. Spread either peanut butter or cream cheese on the rice cake.
4. Make a face by using raisins, peanuts, coconut, or anything else you want.
5. Enjoy it!

Thanksgiving: A seasonal minor interest study

We made a large web chart for the bulletin board with the words WE ARE THANKFUL FOR . . . in the center. I used the overhead projector to draw the original web, which grew as the students thought of more and more things they were thankful for:

mothers, fathers, turkeys, roller skates, bicycles, the sun, spiders, dogs, cats, hamsters, rain, rainbows . . . Two students volunteered to make an enlarged version on paper, using my overhead sheet as a guide. It was a difficult task, but they stuck with it and were proud of their work when I put it up. I also photocopied the overhead so the children would have a copy to take home to share with their parents.

On the Friday before Thanksgiving each child in the whole school brought a lunch from home, decorated with fall leaves, flowers or anything else that caught their fancy. Some lunches were packed in special straw baskets. Luncheon was in the gym, where "buddies" were allowed to sit together. Many of the older buddies had brought something extra for sharing. It's a little hectic in the gym with everyone spread out eating picnic lunches, but it's worth it. We gave our wonderful custodian, Art, a special treat to thank him for the extra work we created for him.

That afternoon we each made a turkey from apples, marshmallows, toothpicks, raisins, and little bits gleaned from our art boxes: felt, buttons, straws . . . These weren't eaten right away. They went home first to decorate Thanksgiving tables.

The day after Thanksgiving we all reported what we had eaten for dinner, then graphed the main courses: 8 turkey dinners, 2 chicken dinners, 2 pizza dinners, 1 hamburger dinner, 1 Chinese dinner, 1 tofu stir-fry dinner. Her classmates knew Morgan was a vegetarian and were interested to hear about her tofu dinner.

For an art project, the students created Thanksgiving dinner placemats. I gave them each a large, stiff rectangular piece of colored paper and asked them to glue a paper plate to the center of it. Then I asked them to draw the things they had used during their dinner — utensils, a napkin, a glass — as if they were looking down on the table; for instance, the glass would be represented by a circle. Then they could add the food they ate, using scraps of paper and anything else they could find. Whatever they used had to be glued on firmly and be light enough so they wouldn't fall off when the "dinners" were pinned to display boards in the classroom and the hall.

Observation

Some conservative souls never want to use anything but a pencil, and some always choose felt pens. So I find that it sometimes helps students stretch their imaginations if we require them to use certain materials or techniques. This time I said, "No pencils, no pens," and the students were inventive in the way they used materials.

Amy used a paper punch to produce her green peas, Thomas used cotton for his mashed potatoes, Ryan found real beans in the math center — not exactly the kind he ate, but close enough. Polly used orange yarn to make spaghetti squash, and Christopher found that thin pieces of foam rubber made good turkey slices. The gravy was brown paint, and guinea pig bedding material ("From the *clean* supply, not the cage, please, Christopher!") was perfect for the stuffing.

Thanksgiving meals also made their way into much of the children's writing during that time. These are a few of my favorites:

Ellen: "We had turkey in Vancouver. We had cranberry and pickles. Their names were Nora and Bino. We had apple pie and ice cream. I had apple juice."

Barbara: "Me and my mother had a turkey dinner. My mom carved the turkey. We also had cooked carrots and also we stuffed the turkey too."

Tessa: "Here's a poem. This is how it goes:
You can eat donuts on Thanksgiving.
You can light the candles.
You can eat pumpkin pie."

Halloween: A favorite minor interest study

I didn't have to do much planning for Halloween. The children started making decorations on their own as the season approached, and soon the room was filled with the usual array of spooks, bats and pumpkins. I simply supplied them with interesting paper and put up a few of my favorite rubber spiders.

We studied a few books and some articles from our nature magazine about spiders and bats. The students were attentive and we all learned a lot, but I didn't notice much interest in an in-depth study of any specific topic. Maybe it was because we'd just recently studied frogs, or perhaps the children were happily involved in their own projects at that time. I left the books I'd collected from the public and school libraries on the classroom shelves so interested students could enjoy them, but abandoned my original research plan.

I usually arrange for some kind of a countdown to Halloween. This year Ellen, who'd been in my class for three years, decided to take charge of that activity. She taught a group of fellow students how to make ghosts from tissues and rubber bands. After each ghost had been numbered, I helped Ellen pin them up on the board, in order. Each day one was removed from the board by the student who had made it, so by Halloween only the "0" was left. Ellen made sure we didn't forget to keep the board up to date.

Marg and I were in charge of the Halloween assembly. We decided to present a few poems and songs, so our classes met several times to select some and learn them together. Representatives from a few other classes volunteered to present skits as well. Everyone in the school dressed up, and we all enjoyed the presentations.

The grade-seven class prepared a Haunted House for their classroom, a tradition at South Park. Some of my students attended, but I didn't encourage them to go. Other years, some have been so frightened that it ruined their whole day — and I'm not willing to crawl through the mazes to keep anyone company! I did that one year and the student and I both ended up backing out, tripping over our long skirts.

Later in the day our two classes went to Beacon Hill Villa, a local retirement home, to sing our songs and talk with the residents. The students had made bookmarks for the seniors, and the seniors enjoyed seeing the children in their costumes. Treats were distributed after our performance.

Our trip to a pumpkin patch the week before Halloween was fun. Each student selected a pumpkin, and we had a tour of the carrot washing and storage facilities.

Back at school, we did a number of related math activities. I divided the children into five groups and gave five pumpkins of varying sizes to each group. Their task was to arrange the five pumpkins in a line according to their weight, no scales allowed. The groups worked together until they thought they had it right, and then we all went around to each table and weighed the pumpkins. They had to shift only a few pumpkins. They had done remarkably well!

Next they worked in small groups to make "circumference collars" for a few of their pumpkins. After they removed the collars, the other groups had to guess which pumpkin each collar would fit. Again we took time to check their predictions.

Finally, the children had a wonderful time carving their own pumpkins, using safety knives — although I did give them help with the lids. At home it's often the parents who plan the face and carve the family jack-o'-lantern. At school the students can carve their faces any way they wish. Because the knives were serrated, the cuts were a little jagged and the resulting features a little fuzzy, but the children didn't mind. Some pumpkins had eyes all the way around, and some had two noses. Kate cut an enormous hole for the mouth, so we could see the entire candle through it. "He's singing," she said.

Some children took their seeds home, but we saved the seeds from two of the pumpkins for some interesting math problems that we made up and talked about together. We counted the seeds by putting them in groups of 10 in muffin papers, and then we set these in lines on the floor, marking off the 100s with colored strips of paper so we could compute the total more easily. The lines turned out to be of greatly different lengths: one pumpkin was decidedly seedier than the other! We called in our principal, Trevor Calkins, to show him what we'd done, since we all knew about his interest in math. He went to find the bathroom scales and helped the students compare their own weight with that of the pumpkins. After he had weighed a number of children, they began to make fairly accurate predictions about how much each next child would weigh.

One of the parents came to the school with an electric frying pan and showed us how to roast some of the seeds for a snack. We also had a very short parent-arranged party in the classroom. The children made pumpkin faces on rice cakes (see page 45), but we decided to skip the cookies, since they'd be getting enough sugar that night while trick-or-treating.

The day after Halloween we worked together to take down our decorations. All of us were happy to get back to our normal routines. I don't think there's another holiday that ends as suddenly and completely as Halloween. It's great while it lasts, but enough is enough.

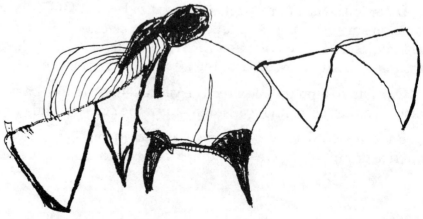

A house in the street: A minor interest study moves in

"There's a house in the street!"

The children came rushing into the room one morning bursting with the news. Since it was blocking both entrances to our parking lot, I had noticed the house earlier myself, but I didn't want to dampen their excitement by telling them so.

"Really? Is there anyone living in it?" I asked.

"No, no," they replied, "It's *stuck*. They were moving it and it got *stuck!* It's too big to get through the trees. They'll have to cut down the trees. Can they do that? Those are our trees!"

"Shall we go out and see it?"

"Oh, yes — you'll see what we mean!"

So we went out. We had a good look at the house and the moving equipment, and we discussed the problem.

"How do you suppose they got those big logs under the house?"

"What is that big crane for?"

"Where is the truck that the branch fell on?"

Would our beautiful chestnut trees really have to lose some branches? We decided that they shouldn't have to be cut down completely. The students proposed solutions:

"Cut the house in half."

"Take off the roof."

"Put it back where it came from."

Some students from the higher grades talked to reporters and to the mayor, who had agreed to come to a meeting with them in the library.

The house stayed all day. We took sketch boards outside so the children could record the event in their drawings. That evening I videotaped the local television news clip about the house so we could watch it together the following day. During the night the unfortunate trees lost some limbs and the house moved on.

The next day we watched the news program and discussed the event again. Excitement was still high. I connected the computer to the large television screen so the students could watch as I typed a story we called "The Day the House Was Stuck on Michigan Street." We decided together which facts to include. Then we made the story more interesting by adding descriptive words and some details to "paint a better picture" for our readers.

The Day the House Was Stuck on Michigan Street
by Linda's class

There was a large old brown wooden house on Michigan Street on Thursday. It was beside South Park School. It was stuck. We had new neighbors!

After our music lesson we went out to see the house. It was huge! One of the big branches they cut fell on the mover's truck.

We liked it when the street was blocked off. We could run to the playground without looking out for cars.

When we went home the house was still there. At night they cut some more branches and moved the house.

We were excited the day the house was stuck on Michigan Street.

Each child received a copy of the story to read with their parents at home, and it was printed in our weekly school newsletter along with several of the students' pencil sketches.

Art gallery trip

I was able to book a tour of the art gallery for late November. Taking the city bus was a great adventure for these car-driven children. Gallery guides took groups of six, each with an accompanying parent, to see the longest painting in the world, a work completed over a period of 36 years by Zhou Zhongfu, a Chinese artist. Depicting the entire length of the Yangtze River, from its origins high in the mountains to its outflow into the sea, the painting went on and on, around and around the rooms for a total of over 30 meters (about 100 feet). The children enjoyed this impressive work very much. They noticed things in the painting that even the museum teachers hadn't seen ("There are sheep next to that little hut, and two of them are goats!") and they asked good questions.

When we returned to the classroom I decided that we might tackle a "longest painting" ourselves. The class across the hall had made a successful one the week before, after their trip, and we had visited their classroom while they were working on it. They called it "The World's *Second* Longest Painting of the Yangtze River." Short visits to other classrooms are often inspiring for children, who are always interested in what other students are doing.

I asked my students if they'd be interested in painting our local Goldstream River, with the spawning of the salmon. Most of them had been to the river at this time of year, either with a preschool group or with their own parents, and we were planning to go there ourselves in a few weeks. I brought out the materials: tempera paints, felt pens and materials for collage. I traced a light line to indicate the position of the river and they spread out on both sides of the long strip of paper to work, adding water, fish, birds, rocks, trees and shrubs to the river scene.

After our trip to Goldstream (see below), I unrolled the painting again and they added things they hadn't included the first time. We voted to send it to the art gallery as a thank-you instead of putting it in the hall or cutting it up to take home.

Salmon: A major interest study

I booked a visit to the Nature House in Goldstream Park and a tour of the stream with a park naturalist. Before we went, we read and discussed some books and articles about the life cycle of the salmon and watched a film. We made a giant circular life-cycle chart to which the students added cutout drawings of the salmon in different stages. We also made several visits to Karen's class upstairs, where they were actually incubating salmon eggs as part of the provincial Salmonid Enhancement Program.

I used this as an opportunity to discuss our human life cycle as well. How different it is from that of the salmon! Or is it?

The naturalist at the Nature House found that the children already knew a good deal about salmon. He taught them more on the banks of the river. We saw mating behavior, a female digging her *redd* (nest) and males fighting to fertilize the eggs. "Why do they want to do that so badly?" asked Jerry — a good question.

Other animals also profit from the salmon run, and the naturalist pointed out some of these as well. For instance:

- The dipper, a small gray bird, "dips" up and down in a peculiar manner and runs along the bottom on the stream looking for salmon eggs.
- Gulls peck at dead salmon. To them, fish eyes are a gourmet treat.

The children watched the naturalist dissect a salmon that was still heavy with eggs. They were interested to see what was inside the fish. He even showed us the brain! We later wrote him a nice thank-you letter with some interesting illustrations.

Back in the classroom, the students completed individual copies of a small booklet I had written. Each page told a little about one stage of salmon development: *egg, eyed egg, alevin, fry, adult salmon* and *spawning salmon*. The children practiced reading the pages and illustrated them in their own wonderful styles, then proudly took the booklets home to share with their parents.

I announced that the following day would be "project day." My students are always excited about project days, when they get the entire morning to work on a project of their choice. I love those days too, because I have a chance to see how wonderfully creative the children can be and how much they learned from a field trip or study. Project days always remind me how very important the outings we take together are for stimulating my students' imagination and teaching them about the real world. Of course they also give me a splendid opportunity to write some good assessment notes about individual students.

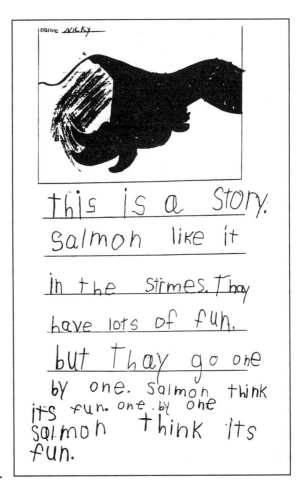

name NICKY

this is a story. Salmon like it in the stimes. Thay have lots of fun. but thay go one by one. Salmon think its fun. one by one Salmon think its fun.

Overnight — consciously or subconsciously — most of the students had done some planning, as shown by the variety of projects they embarked on in class the next day:

- Some wrote individual books.
- One small group created a puppet play which they presented to our class in the morning and to two other classes in the afternoon.
- Using paper rolls, cardboard and small pink beads, two boys made a three-dimensional model of a salmon laying eggs.
- One girl made a model of part of the Nature House.
- Many made drawings of what they'd seen from the banks of the stream and then wrote about the pictures.
- One used the word processor to compose "the longest story I've even written."

Before lunch they all shared their work with each other on the carpet. After each presentation, the other students asked questions and told the artists or writers what they liked about their work. Then the presenter was given a round of applause. If I ever forget to orchestrate applause, either the presenter or one of the other students reminds me that "we didn't do the clapping." It must be important to them.

In the afternoon the half-day students were given an opportunity to discuss the morning projects with the all-day students and do short projects of their own, since they had participated in the field trip as well. Usually we invite our half-day students to come for the entire day when events such as these are planned.

Student-led conferences: A successful experiment

NOTE: For background reading, see *Evaluation: A Team Effort* (pages 25-26), *On the Move* (pages 303-307) and *Student-Led Teacher-Parent Conferences*.

Marg and I decided to hold student-led conferences instead of traditional parent-teacher conferences. We obtained permission from the parents and the principal and made a schedule and agenda. Then we worked with our students to help them prepare for the conference day, when they would be explaining their school programs to their parents and demonstrating the progress they'd made in their studies.

The parents later told us how impressed they were by their young children's ability to articulate their own progress and explain their plans for improving in different areas. We weren't surprised, however. We realized how many skills our students had used as they prepared for and held the conferences, how much more self-confident they had become, and how deeply they had benefited by being intimately involved in their own evaluation. This kind of experience helps children understand that they are, at least in part, responsible for their own education.

Plant growth: A long-term minor interest study

Jamie's mother Patryck is a gardener who is often free to come into my classroom to help out. I have many fuchsia plants at home, so I asked her if she'd be interested in taking charge of a fuchsia-grown-from-clippings project. It would give the children something special to give to their parents during the holiday season. She agreed and bought the necessary cups, vermiculite, soil and rooting compound. One afternoon she arrived with those and I brought in my clippings. She gave the whole class a talk about the procedures and then took the children a group at a time to do the planting, while the others enjoyed activity time.

About once a week she'd return to show the children how the roots were developing. In a few weeks they were ready to be transplanted into larger pots with potting soil. Each child did his or her own plant, and then we put them all in special trays in the sand table to watch them grow. By mid-December they were ready to be wrapped in hand-printed paper and taken home to be presented as gifts. Most of the plants survived that experience, and I had a few extras to replace those that didn't. Jamie took one home for Patryck, of course, and she was dutifully pleased.

After the fuschia plants got started I brought in this year's amaryllis bulb. The amaryllis is a wonderful plant — once the shoot emerges from the bulb, it grows so fast you can almost see it climb! Almost every year my class watches one grow, and even second- and third-year students never tire of this study.

The students helped me plant the bulb. After giving it its first watering, we recorded our guesses about what color the flower would be and how high the plant would grow. We decided to measure the tallest stem once a week and keep track of its growth on a graph.

The children helped me prepare a graph on a chart-sized piece of graph paper. We labeled it appropriately, using the horizontal axis for dates and the vertical axis for growth in centimeters. I wanted to allow room to record one meter (over three feet) of growth, so we had to count the squares on the paper and plan how many centimeters each square would represent. We found that each square could represent two centimeters (a bit less than an inch), and I wrote the numbers lightly on the lines. Then we used our calendar to determine which dates we should write along the bottom of the graph. Finally, Ryan traced over my penciled numbers with a thin black pen. Letting the class help set up the graph was much better than just appearing one morning with one ready to use. The students felt more a part of the project, they understood the concept better, and they saw the thought processes that were necessary to complete the job.

Each week a different child measured and recorded the growth of our plant while the rest of us watched. Another volunteered to add to the drawing of the emerging plant that was "growing" alongside the line on the graph. I had never asked my students to draw a plant alongside a graph before, but it worked quite well. It looked wonderful and I think this addition helped the students understand much better how a line graph works. A graph can be rather mysterious to a six-year-old.

The plant was also measured unofficially many times a day, by many students. Jamie was especially keen: he raced for the plant first thing each morning, almost before he said a word to anyone, and announced how much it had grown during the night.

Observation

I had given a bulb to Marg as well, thinking that it would be fun to see which plant would bloom first. We could have a little friendly competition and meet to compare graphs and plants each week. It didn't work out, however. Her bulb just *sat* there while ours shot up and bloomed. Not much of a competition! Just as our last flower was forming, theirs began to grow. Obviously a late-bloomer . . . and another lesson for the late-bloomers in the class!

As our blossoms began to unfold, we discovered that they were a beautiful shade of scarlet. There were six magnificent flowers in all, on three separate stems. What to do with such a beautiful plant?

Photograph it, of course, and bring out the paper and paint. I put out charcoal, oil pastels and felt pens as well. The students could choose one medium, mix two or more media, or try many different pictures using different media each time. There was no problem with motivation. This was their plant. They had watched it develop for weeks and welcomed the opportunity to record it in their art.

Observation

Jason, a young student whose low self-esteem was causing the usual social problems, became really involved with this project. He covered many papers with beautiful images of the amaryllis. It was wonderful to see him expressing a different side of himself. His classmates noticed his fine work too. I could feel his pride when I added his pictures to the impressive array of artwork that filled our bulletin boards.

The drawings, the graph and the plant itself (now beginning to fade) formed one of the centers for our student-led conferences in mid-December. There was lots to talk about, and the parents were given an introduction to how productive integrated studies can be.

Hanukkah: A cultural minor interest study

Over the years I've collected a number of good stories, several songs and many enjoyable activities about Hanukkah, the Jewish Festival of Light. Overwhelmed as our culture is with Christmas, it's important for children to become aware of other customs and appreciate different religions. Participating in Hanukkah activities helps my students do that. And they're fun! This year Marg and I worked together to prepare enough activities for two days.

Our classes assembled to hear the story of Hanukkah and learn some songs. I told rather than read the story: the invasion of the Greek soldiers, the destruction of the Temple, the forced worship, the flight to the mountains, the guerrilla warfare and then the final trimuph, with the rededication of the Temple and the miracle of the oil. Afterwards we divided the students into two groups, mixing the two classes so that everyone would have a chance to work with peers they didn't see every day. Those who stayed with me did two things.

First, they worked in small groups to calculate how many candles would be required to complete the menorah ceremony for the eight days of Hanukkah. This required sophisticated mathematical thinking: two candles the first night, three the next, and so forth for eight days. I distributed toothpick "candles" they could use to help them do their calculations, independently or with friends. The students who understood quickly were soon surrounded by classmates who were confused and wanted some help. After a certain amount of time we all met on the carpet to discuss the results. They had come up with many different numbers: 9, 36, 48, 54 . . .!

When I asked volunteers to describe the techniques they'd used to arrive at their figures, different children explained how they had drawn their menorahs and set up their "candles" to figure out their answers. While describing their thought processes, some of the students realized that they had forgotten to take one thing or another into consideration, so their numbers weren't right. I was fascinated by the number of approaches they'd used.

Then, using a large drawing of a menorah and real menorah candles, we all worked together to discover the correct number. Our "burned up" candles went into a pile and we counted them after we'd completed the ceremony together. The answer? Forty-four.

The second activity centered on art. We looked at pictures of different menorahs and at two or three real ones that had been brought into the classroom. Although every one was different, we noticed that they all had nine candleholders: eight grouped together and one set apart. The students' assignment was to design a menorah that followed this pattern. They could draw one and cut it out, or use Plasticine, playdough or any other art materials. I put their creative and varied finished products either on a bulletin board or on a shelf in a special corner of the room.

In her classroom Marg helped the children make latkes, the traditional Hanukkah potato pancakes, and applesauce to go with them. She had arranged for a parent who celebrates Hanukkah with her family to help her. When they were finished, they enjoyed their food and listened to the parent read relevant stories and tell about how Hanukkah is celebrated in their home. Sol, her son, was pleased to share his family's customs with the class.

Hanukkah Latkes

2 large potatoes ½ onion 225 mL / 1 cup flour 5 mL / 1 tsp. salt oil	Equipment: grater, frypan, mixing bowl, spoon, spatula, measuring cup, peeler

Peel and grate the potatoes and the onion.
Add flour and salt.
Mix thoroughly until smooth.
Grease the frying pan.
Drop the batter into the hot pan, making each pancake about 8 cm (3") in diameter.
Fry until brown on both sides.
Remove from the frying pan and drain on paper towels.

Serve with a little applesauce on each one.

The next day I taught both classes how to play the *dreydl* game, another good math activity. The children learned the rules by watching four students who played as I taught. Then we formed groups of six so everyone had a chance to participate.

The game requires a dreydl, a spinning top with Hebrew letters printed on the four sides: *nun, gimmel, hay* and *shin*. The players spin the dreydl and read the symbols, which tell them what to do with the pile of pennies they're trying to accumulate from the main pile in the middle of the circle: *nun*, do nothing; *gimmel*, take all of the pennies from the main pile; *hay*, take half of the pennies from the main pile; *shin*, give up your pile. After each child's turn, everyone donates one penny to the main pile.

For several days afterwards, both Marg and I left the instructions and the necessary equipment at one of our activity centers so the students could play on their own during activity time.

I also read aloud a story by Mary Dodson Wade called "Crystal Candles," which I found in an old *Highlights for Children* magazine. It tells how Moishe, a boy whose mother had to sell their beautiful silver menorah after his father's death, made a paper menorah and taped it to the window. On Hanukkah, Moishe's mother gave him a warm winter coat she had recut from one that had belonged to her husband, and he gave her a note promising to sweep the stairs for her every day. She was so happy with this gift that when we talked about it afterwards we decided to do something similar for members of our own families. We listed possible promises of service the children could offer:

- help wash the car or the dishes
- take out the garbage
- clean my room without being asked
- take the dog for a walk every day
- try not to fight with my sister/brother
- change the hamster cage without being asked

Some of the students suggested that the promises should be more specific — they didn't want to have to take out the garbage or wash the dishes *forever*, and would this mean that other family members wouldn't have to walk the dog? I told them they could write their promises any way they wanted. And they did.

On our weekly buddy day, all of us went into the gym to dance the *hora*, a traditional Jewish dance. I played the piano while the children danced in a huge circle. Neither Marne, the buddy-class teacher, nor I really knew the steps, but the students invented their own and we all had a great time.

Parents often tell me that they appreciate such things as our Hanukkah study. Non-Jewish parents are happy that their children are given an opportunity to understand more about another way of life in such an enjoyable and meaningful way. Jewish parents are happy that their children have a chance to feel proud of their heritage.

A taste of Japan: An unexpected visitor

The day we began our Hanukkah study a young teacher from Japan appeared at our school. She could speak a little English, and she wanted to observe a classroom in action in Canada. Marg and I welcomed her and asked her if she'd like to help out with our Hanukkah celebration. She watched the children work and spoke a little with them while she completed a beautiful drawing of a menorah which she had offered to provide for our math problem with the candles. In the afternoon she read a Japanese story to the students. She also wrote each of their names in Japanese characters. Some of the children rushed to the tables to practice making their own names, and some used Japanese characters when they wrote their names on their writing workshop papers for several days afterwards.

Our visitor seemed to enjoy her day with us and at the same time taught us a bit about yet another culture. We wondered what she thought of our classes, so different from those in Japan!

The winter concert: A class event

What to do for this year's winter concert? During one of our family meetings the parents and I decided that we would have a finger food potluck dinner before the performance. Maureen, one of the parents who works backstage in a local theater, offered to help with costumes for the performance itself.

Observation

Experience has taught me to aim for a presentation filled with the students' own ideas and not requiring hours of rehearsal time. Disrupting routine classroom activities too often becomes hard on the children. Extensive rehearsals usually produce discipline problems, a sure sign that something isn't right. I also have to think of the audience. Young children don't always project their voices well, particularly when they are terrified!

Since they hadn't yet participated in any whole-class drama activities, I asked the students if they'd like to put on a play. They said they would, so I read them several fairy tales and helped them think about how we could present each one. We settled on *The Emperor's New Clothes*. I read two different versions and we selected the one we liked best. After we listed the characters on the board, each student chose a part. The entire half-day group was to be "the crowd in the street," and some of the more timid all-day students chose to join them.

Both Tessa and Christopher wanted to be the Emperor. Someone suggested that they could be married, so we changed the play to *The Emperor's and the Empress's New Clothes*.

Maureen brought in heaps of old dress-up clothes, jewels, belts and hats, and the children selected their own costumes, after a lot of discussion and bargaining. Another parent provided long-john pajamas for the royal couple. The weavers, the thieves, the crowd, all thought about what props they were going to need, and somehow they appeared. Morgan showed up one day with a dog costume left over from Halloween. She had decided that dogs would have been present in the crowd, even in those days. She let different children take turns holding her leash during the performance. That little bit of activity was an added interest for the audience — I wasn't even aware that it had happened until afterwards!

I revised the text to include the Empress and read it aloud for both the rehearsals and the performance itself, while the students acted it out. They had to practice their entrances and exits and learn how to stand on stage so their parents could see their faces, but other than that, we didn't spend much time perfecting the play. They didn't have to memorize much dialogue because I was narrating the story. There were a few big moments, however. Jamie's came when he, a boy in the crowd, had to remember to say, "But they aren't wearing any clothes!" He came through beautifully. His mother, a self-confessed sentimentalist, watched her son through her tears.

The play was a huge success. When you work with a group of young children, successful performances are guaranteed if you let them contribute their ideas and if you don't expect perfection. Even their mistakes are taken in stride by the audience.

The planning and presentation of *The Emperor's and the Empress's New Clothes* involved the children in a variety of activities in many of the different academic, emotional, physical and social domains. A day or two after the event, for instance, I gave them a writing assignment: "Write about what part you had in the play, including at least one thing that you did or said. Tell what you liked best about our play, and tell how you felt about being in it."

The students all completed the assignment, at their own levels. Some used "pretend writing," others included many real letters, and some used a good deal of

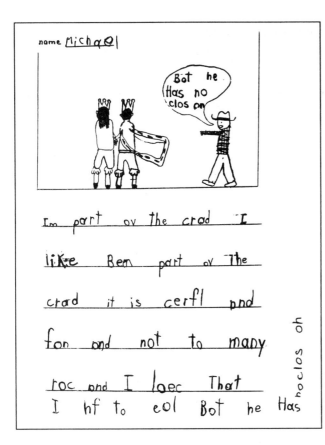

standard spelling. When they were finished, they came to me and read their work aloud as I typed on the word processor. If I didn't understand something, I sent the student back to his or her seat to add to the sentences or paragraphs that were incomplete. The half-day students dictated their changes to me. Since they were still using pretend writing, there was no point in asking them to write more!

I printed the text on the classroom printer and put together a book with each child's essay on a separate page. Above their own writing I asked them to produce black-line drawings of themselves in the play. When these were complete I photocopied the book so each would have a copy to take home as a souvenir for themselves and their parents.

Observation

Many of the children were eager to try to read what they and their friends had written about our play. One parent told me that her daughter actually taught herself to read using these school-produced booklets! Here are some examples of their writing:

Tessa: "I'm the Empress. We practiced our play. We got some clothes and jewelry. I like the play. I get to wear some long-johns and they tell me about the cloth. My favorite part is when I take off my dress."

Janet: "I am the Empress's assistant. I go into the room where the five weavers are working. I said, "They are beautiful. What rich colors. It's lovely.""

Michael: "I'm part of the crowd. I like being part of the crowd. It is cheerful and fun and not too much work and I like that. I have to yell, 'But he has no clothes on!'"

Ryan: "I was part of the crowd. I was watching the Emperor and the Empress. I said, 'Oh, look at the wonderful clothes.' I said it louder and louder."

Science experiments: An unexpected major interest study begins

One morning in January I walked back in after recess to find two girls busily at work at one of the tables and a group of their classmates watching them with interest. They were mixing earth with water in a big bowl. They explained that they were scientists experimenting with mud. Kate said, "We add a little water and mix and see what happens, then we add more water to see what happens next. Isn't it neat?"

I quickly decided it would be a good time to set up a science experiment in the classroom. If they found mud interesting, I was sure they'd be interested in an experiment with more dramatic results!

The next day I poured 150 mL (⅔ cup) of salad oil into a graduated glass cylinder and slid in an ice cube. It floated, of course. I put the container in the center of the carpet and we all lay down in a circle to watch. The predictions varied widely: "It will sink." . . . "It will just stay the same." . . . "It will melt." . . . "The oil will freeze." We watched for a long time, experienced the unpredicted, and then wrote up the experiment on the board. We listed the materials we used, explained the steps we took, and told what happened. When we were finished I asked each student to draw a picture depicting the "ice cube in oil" experiment and write about it in their own words. They were to take these papers home so they could follow their own instructions when they repeated the experiment for their siblings or parents.

They were so enthusiastic about doing more experiments that I went to work to prepare a "science experiment month." From the many books of experiments I found in the school and public libraries I selected about 30 experiments of different types, all of which could be completed in about 10 minutes using readily available materials. I spread photocopies out on the tables and invited the children to circulate to look at them and then gather on the carpet. Using the chance box to determine the order, I asked individuals to return to the tables to select the experiment they would like to perform for the class. As usual, some were disappointed when a friend chose the experiment they wanted, but they all believed our selection system was fair, so they were good sports about choosing another. The most desirable ones, predictably, were the baking-soda-and-vinegar volcano and the exploding cork.

When all the selections had been made, I asked each student to choose a date for their "Scientist of the Day" presentation. These would be held in the afternoons, two each day, so the half-day students could participate. We wrote the names on our calendar.

The note that went home with a copy of the experiment asked the parents to please help their child gather the materials and practice, so he or she would know what to say and do when the big day arrived.

For the presentations, the "scientist" donned a white lab coat with a SCIENTIST button on the lapel and performed the experiment in the "amphitheater" I had made in the classroom with chairs. The audience was always attentive and interested. During the discussions that followed, class members suggested theories about why certain things had happened during the course of an experiment. The students frequently drew connections between this experiment and those they'd seen on other days: "That's what happened in Mary's experiment, but she used balloons, not magnets!" They also suggested other things that could be tried with the same materials, wondering "What would happen if . . .?"

Observation

We watched as Morgan's drop of liquid soap caused grains of floating pepper to rush to the sides of the dish. We saw Nicky's candle go out when she covered it with an overturned glass. We were amazed when Amy's cork hit the ceiling and when Thomas's paper boat moved across the water, propelled by vinegar and baking soda. We marveled when Barbara's peeled egg plopped into the narrow neck of a jar. We were interested to see, when Jamie tested them with iodine, which foods contained starch. We continued to ask Janet to repeat her volcano experiment until she ran out of baking soda and the smell of vinegar filled the hallway.

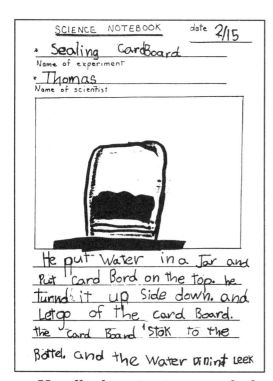

Usually the scientist was asked to perform the experiment more than once, and we never forgot to give him or her an enthusiastic round of applause. Sometimes the parents came along to watch their budding scientist at work, but they were not allowed to help. Not one child forgot to bring in the necessary supplies on the appointed day!

Observation

I had given each child a "science notebook" with 25 blank pieces of paper and had asked everyone to write up each experiment. At the top of the page I asked them to print the date, the name of the scientist and the name of the experiment, which I had written on the board. They were to complete a drawing and to write about it in any way they wanted to.

Depending on their attention span and their level of development, they wrote a lot or a little, some with care and others quickly, some in standard or temporary spelling and others in pretend writing. Here are some entries made after we saw Ryan's electromagnet experiment:

Christopher: "Ryan did a science experiment. It is an electromagnet. First he took out a big battery, wire, and a nail. Then he picked up the nail and touched it to the paper clip. It was an electromagnet!"

Robert: "1. Gaet a batrey and waire.
2. Waind up one end of the waire.
3. pot a nael into the tewrn of waire.
4. Aatash the ans of the waire to the batrey.
5. Then it is a lacktomagnt."

Tessa: "Today Ryan did a sims expamt. Wh you hook the wir on the badri the nie shd make a mant and Then you shd beabl to pak ap paprkls."

Michael: "Ryan did a siens exsperament it was OSEM! It was cald ELECTROMAGNET. frst He pot the woers on the speings Then you pot the nael on and Then you put on the metl."

Carol: "1. T M A L P   Kate:
2. T L J
3. L J T Mqi0
4. FJ nb!"

The science notebooks, all different, were very interesting and colorful. This was a successful interest study — at the end of it, the children all agreed that they "love science!" It also gave me a good opportunity to do some meaningful assessment of my students' speaking and writing skills, and of their attitudes and interests.

A science experiment for students to perform for and discuss with their parents was one of the centers for the student-led conferences. The children shared their science notebooks with their parents at that time as well.

Polar bears: A student-inspired minor interest study

January brought a lot of snow, much to the delight of the students. We took advantage of the unusual Victoria weather by going for walks in the park, writing snow poems together, building snow forts on the playground and learning about negative temperatures.

Ellen's thoughts turned to polar bears. On the bus she asked one of the teaching assistants, Katie, whether polar bear babies were born under water or on land. Katie didn't know, so she relayed the question to me. I wasn't sure either, and none of the children knew, so I asked Ellen to go to the library (the usual starting place when we need information) to see what she could find, with the help of our librarian.

The next day *Ranger Rick*, the nature magazine we subscribe to, arrived with a feature story about polar bears! Happily, we found the answer to Ellen's question: the mother bears dig snow caves in which their guinea-pig sized babies are born in January or February — right when we were reading about them! I asked the class if they'd like to learn more about these animals. They said they were interested, so we read some more books and I ordered a film from the media center. I knew the commentary would be above their heads, but it had some interesting footage of polar bears in their natural environment. I helped them understand some of the language.

I thought it might be a good time for me to introduce them to report writing as well. I'd had a successful experience using the following technique with a previous class when we studied octopuses (see *The Learners' Way*, pages 223-227), so I decided to try it again.

I wrote headings on five different charts:
- How Polar Bears Look
- How Polar Bears Move
- What Polar Bears Eat
- How Polar Bears Hunt
- Other Interesting Facts about Polar Bears

Whenever we learned something new, I wrote it down in note form on the appropriate chart. We had already learned quite a bit, so we were able to start taking notes right away. We had some interesting discussions about where certain facts should be written. Should the fact that they hear very well go under "Other Interesting Facts" or "How Polar Bears Look"?

By the time we were finished, this is what had been written under "How Polar Bears Hunt":
- chase prey under the sea — swim fast
- on ice, sneak up and pounce on seals
- from water, jump onto ice to get seals
- wait near seal breathing holes
- dig under ice to get baby seals

Observation

Jamie had suggested the last one. "Jamie," I said, "are you sure? I don't remember reading about that." "Yes!" he said. "I'll show you." He went to find the book he had been looking at during reading time and pointed to a cutaway drawing of a polar bear digging through the ice to penetrate a seal's den. Jamie couldn't read the text, but he had read the picture and contributed to our research. He was very proud.

My idea had been to show the class how these notes could be written in sentences to create different chapters in a book. I noticed, however, that their interest had fallen off sharply, and I was afraid I was going to have to work too hard to keep their attention. Last year's "octopus class" had been further along academically and, as a whole, the students had been able to concentrate for longer periods of time. Since my current students had already done quite a bit of directed writing in their science notebooks, I realized that they probably needed time to pursue their own interests. I knew, too, that many of them weren't really ready for such advanced written work.

I decided to give them a choice: work with me to complete the book (a project I described in glowing terms), or complete a project of their own choice — on their own or with one or two friends — about snow, polar bears, or other animals or people who live in the snow. Most chose the independent projects. While they got to work, I worked with my four volunteers.

The five of us had a good time together. We read the notes the class had made and decided how we'd write each chart up as a different chapter. They watched as I used the word processor, and we all made editorial suggestions. Morgan suggested that the "How Polar Bears Hunt" chapter should come before the "What Polar Bears Eat." That made sense. For the former we wrote:

> Polar bears hunt in many ways. Sometimes they wait patiently near the breathing holes seals make in the ice. When a seal comes up to breathe, the bear grabs it. Other times they sneak up on the seals while they are resting on the ice. They can move very quietly. Sometimes they jump out of the water onto a seal that is on the ice. In the sea, they can swim very fast while chasing fish or seals. Polar bears can dig through the ice to reach baby seals in their dens.

When we had finished, the students and I read the completed chapters to the class. I made a Big Book, using the text I had produced on the printer and enlarged on the photocopier, and they went to work illustrating the pages. We added a title page that listed Morgan, Nicky, Ellen, Janet and me as authors and gave credit to the rest of the class for helping with the research. We added a table of contents and a bibliography. Each student in the class was given a copy of the "Polar Bear Book" to take home, and the Big Book became part of our class library.

Valentine's Day: A social event

The previous year on Valentine's Day we had gone to sing at Beacon Hill Villa, a retirement home around the corner where we go several times a year. When the social director gave me a call to arrange a time for this year, I told her I would ask the children to make Valentines for the residents. She thought this was a good idea and said that they'd have treats for us. I knew the children would be getting plenty of treats elsewhere, so I asked her if she thought her residents would like to make Valentines for my students instead. "Would the children like that?" she asked. Of course they would!

We decided that she'd drop off a list containing the names of the people who wanted to participate and I'd assign a student partner to each, either from my class or from Christine's primary class, and return a copy of the list to her. There were just the right number: 46 in all. It was much more fun planning our visit when we knew the names of the people we were going to see. The children speculated about what their Valentines would look like.

They put themselves wholeheartedly into their card making. A parent had brought in a discarded book of wedding invitation sample cards she'd been given (a good source for hearts, flowers and birds), we had some ribbon from somewhere, we bought doilies and glitter, and we had some good red tagboard — offcuts from our local printers. The Valentines were magnificent, of course. We affixed stickers with the names of the partners so the cards wouldn't be mixed up.

Christine and I knew that some of the partner meetings would be more successful than others, since some of the Villa residents have a difficult time communicating for one reason or another. Some can't hear, some can't see, some have lost a lot of their mental ability. So, before we went we did a bit of playacting to give our students some idea about what they might encounter, what they might say, and how they might act if their Valentine partner wasn't very responsive.

The children looked forward to our outing, and when we arrived it looked as if the residents had been waiting eagerly as well. First we sang our songs. We began with one Christine had made up and followed with one we knew the residents would also enjoy, the old favorite *Side by Side*. Some of them joined in as we sang it three times.

Then the social director showed the children where their Valentines were sitting. We watched as the children shyly made their way to find their partners, cards in hand. Some of them had touching conversations with the old people — there are some children who seem to have a knack for communicating. Polly went right up to Mrs. Beardsley and held her hand while she chatted on about her hamster and her new bicycle. Some, predictably, weren't able to get much response. The nurses helped them out the best they could. "My Valentine didn't even know I was there," Eric told me. "Well, you never know," I told him. "Maybe she listened and was really happy but couldn't show you because she'd had a stroke or some other problem. Maybe this was the best day she had in a long time."

The boys and girls left the cards they had made, said thank-you for the cards they had received, waved goodbye to their Valentines and went quietly back to join their classmates. We sang our song again and then returned to school. I kept the list of names. Some of the children said they wanted to continue making things for their new friends.

Back at school, we had an assembly and a short party and Valentine exchange for ourselves. Our trip to Beacon Hill Villa, however, was the highlight of that day.

Chinese New Year: A planned minor interest study

For the last few years I've walked my students and many of their parents to a pleasant restaurant in Chinatown around the time of the Chinese New Year. At a small cost, they provide us with a lunch composed of dishes they know children like. Some students try to use their chopsticks, but most end up with forks. The owners give the children little red "good luck" envelopes and fortune cookies at the end of the meal. I make sure that our thank-you letter is especially well written and beautifully decorated, since I know it will be posted by the front door and may stay there for months!

Back in the classroom after this year's trip, we studied the 12-year cycle of the Chinese calendar. The students went home armed with a chart to find out the birth years of their parents, grandparents and friends so they could determine the appropriate animal signs. "Both of my parents are *horses*," Barbara announced, "and my grandmother is a *monkey*!" The information was displayed on a graph the students helped to complete.

As part of our Chinese New Year study we read books about Chinese culture, looked at books written in Chinese, and listened to a Chinese speaker (a friend of Ted's parents), who also read a book he had read to his own children when they were small. We talked about the way some of the Chinese characters came to be written. There are some good children's books on the subject. I gave the students strips of red paper, soft brushes and black paint so they could practice making the characters themselves. Some of them made up their own characters and some enjoyed copying those printed in books or in the Chinese newspapers I distributed.

That was enough exposure for most of the students, and we went on to something else. However, Thomas was really intrigued by the idea of symbols standing for whole words instead of sounds. For several days during activity time he drifted to the writing books and newspapers and practiced drawing characters. He made up characters of his own, and even made up a short story using his invented characters! Occasionally I've had students use invented spelling to write the French we'd been learning, but I'd never before seen one invent sentences in Chinese!

Castles: A major interest study emerges

The students had been busy doing their own writing, following their own interests and enjoying our normal, busy classroom routines, but we hadn't worked on a major study together since we'd completed the science experiments in January. It was time, I decided, to provide some needed stimulation and a fresh focus to help them develop new skills. "Let's transform the playhouse again," I suggested. The children agreed enthusiastically. No one was using the library we'd set up there and they wanted something more exciting.

We brainstormed ideas and narrowed our choices to four that at least two students wanted: a restaurant, a police station, a school or a castle. Once everyone had selected one of these options, the groups met to plan a strategy for convincing their classmates to vote for their ideas, and to prepare their presentations. They could write up their speeches, or they could make notes or draw pictures to remind them of their arguments. After about 20 minutes of preparation, we held a class meeting and the groups presented in turn.

◆ "We should have a *restaurant*," said Nicky, when it was her group's turn. "We could put up pretty tables and chairs and we could make playdough food and make menus." Tessa added, "We could have a cash register."

- "We want it to be a *police station*," argued Michael. "We could have weapons and walkie-talkies, ghost cars and sirens." Robert added, "We could make cars out of boxes that we could put on to pretend we were going to catch robbers. I could bring in my handcuffs."

- "It would be nice to have a *school*," said Christopher. "We could pretend to go on field trips. It would be fun to be a teacher or a student. It's never been a school before." Janet added, "We could take in our pens and we could draw, and it would be funny because sometimes the kids would be taller than the teacher."

- It should be a *castle*," said Sonja. "I like castles because you can dress up. I like princesses and knights." Jerry added, "We can make armor and have sword fights."

After the presentations I explained the concept of a secret ballot. I passed out pieces of paper and the students all went to different corners of the room to write down their selections. We used the chance box to select two students: Thomas to read the ballots and Kate to tabulate the results on the board. Castles won by a landslide, and we got to work right away.

We went to the library to check out as many books as we could find about castles, and the children brought books from home to add to the collection. A parent went to the public library to search for additional books. Some students brought swords and shields, models of knights and other objects from home. Michael spent some of his own money at a neighborhood garage sale to buy an andiron in the shape of a knight. Amy brought some postcards and a large poster showing the inside of a castle. Sarah had been to Scotland the previous summer, where she had collected postcards of all of the castles she visited. I let her set up a station at a table so she could call her classmates to view them in groups of two or three. Nicky's mother grew up in Austria, so she was able to bring in a large book of photographs of Austrian castles to share with us. We had many good discussions about different aspects of castle construction and castle life. When we came to their toilet facilities, we even touched on the importance of hygiene in preventing the spread of disease.

I had been given some extra classroom money, so I bought the Playmobil castle, which my college-age son Carl helped us put together. The students developed a sign-up procedure for organizing playtime with the castle, using the chalkboard to list groups of players and the timer to signal the end of each group's turn.

We looked at our books and talked about what we could do to make the playhouse look like a castle. We decided that it needed battlements, a moat and a drawbridge. It should be made of stones, or at least painted gray. I provided extra materials from our school art cupboard: tagboard, paint rollers and a large piece of corrugated cardboard for the drawbridge. I also found some rope at home after our yarn broke after just two bridge-raisings.

While part of the class was busy with this project, another group was particularly keen to make armor. The students worked all morning cutting cardboard and working out ways to attach the sections and get the parts to fit properly. The planning and helping and pride of accomplishment were wonderful! The blisters on their fingers caused by using their little scissors to cut cardboard were badges they accepted with courage.

Others worked on the inside of the castle. What was missing? We moved in a table and a rug. What did they have for decorations in those days? We did some more research and found that they had tapestries and banners and that they often hung up their shields on the walls, or at least had paintings of shields and such. These discoveries led to art projects. In our books we noticed all the different shapes shields could have. Each student made his or her own shield shape out of tagboard and then applied designs with a printing process I demonstrated for them, using styrofoam meat trays, paint and rollers. Another day they worked in pairs to paint tapestries, using large pieces of paper suspended from sticks. Some chose to make flags or banners instead.

One day I divided the class into groups of three or four to work on small castles using material from the all-important art junk box. I bought extra tape for the occasion. This time I didn't give them a choice about who was to be in each group — I wanted them to develop some new friendships and learn to work with many different children. I tried to let them solve their own problems without my guidance, and while they planned and worked together I took notes about their interactions.

Observation

One very creative girl who had always had trouble working cooperatively discovered that her group could accomplish a lot in a short time if she worked with the others instead of insisting on having her own way. It was a breakthrough for her, and a real learning experience.

The children worked hard on this project all morning, and just before lunch we shared the results with the class from across the hall. The members of each group explained what they had done.

"Our castle has a drawbridge that goes up instead of dropping down."

"This strawberry basket is the dungeon. There is a tunnel you can't see that connects it to the castle."

"Our castle has two towers. It was really hard to make the flag stand up straight."

We all admired their castles and found positive things to say about each one. The students asked the architects some very interesting questions. I had the same two questions for each group, and they never failed to elicit interesting answers: "Did you have any problems?" and "How did you solve them?"

The next day I asked the students to draw a picture of the castle they helped build and write about it, in much the same way as they had written about their parts in the winter play (see pages 58-59). I insisted that they include at least the following information:

◆ Who was in the group?
◆ What part did you work on?

- What part or parts were the most difficult?
- What did you find interesting about the castle?

I told them they could use invented spelling, since I was planning to type their work on the word processor using standard spelling and punctuation. After they'd all finished writing and I'd typed their pieces, they illustrated them and we put them together into a charming book called "Our Castles."

The playhouse castle became the setting for a lot of dramatic play, particularly for the younger children. Fighting with plastic swords was the obvious activity for young knights. I wondered about allowing it, but since they were having such a good time and no one was getting hurt, I decided they could go ahead — if they could keep the noise level down. They found that they could, especially once they realized that I really would ask them to leave if they continued to be noisy after a warning!

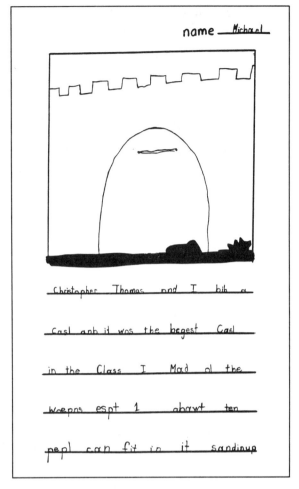

This study lasted about a month. We didn't work actively on it every day, although some students chose to write about castles and knights almost daily during their writing workshop time, and some spent a lot of time working on armor during activity time. Not everything we did revolved around castles, of course. Some of the bulletin boards displayed unrelated student art and writing, and although we read many books about castles, we also enjoyed books about other things.

We all learned a lot about castles during that month, however, myself included. I find that learning new things along with the children is one of the most enjoyable aspects of teaching in a holistic classroom.

Mother's Day: A personal minor study interest study

Mother's Day was approaching, and I wanted my students to create very personal gifts for their mothers.

I remembered that during a recent math lesson involving graphing they'd really enjoyed interviewing their classmates to gather information about favorite pets and colors. So I devised a "My Mom" questionnaire for them to take home and complete by interviewing their mothers about their interests, their favorite activities and some personal history. Part of the questionnaire included statements like these:

My mom has ____ children.

My mom likes to do this with me: _____.

When my mom was little she wanted to grow up to be _____.

My mom grew up in _____.

In a note, I suggested to the mothers that they might want to help with the reading, spelling and printing because there was a lot to write and I wanted to be sure that either the author or the author's teacher would be able to read the completed questionnaire at school! The students and their mothers all enjoyed the interview process. A girl who was staying with her father at the time questioned her mom on the phone.

I interviewed my own mother too, so I could share the answers with my students and demonstrate how I used her responses to create sentences for my own "My Mom" book.

When the papers came back, my more advanced scholars wrote their own booklets. Another adult or I worked with the rest of the children individually, reading their notes with them and helping them decide which facts they wanted to include in their books. Some printed their own sentences; others asked us to scribe for them. The books were lovingly illustrated by the authors and made nice personal gifts for their mothers.

Observation

Christopher read his own notes and wrote: "My mom is 44. My mom has 2 children. She likes to dance, write, do yoga and garden. My mom likes to play, talk, walk and read with me. She wanted to grow up to be a horseback rider. Mom likes the way lilacs smell and look. She likes to read poetry and psychology books. Mom wants to go on a vacation in Mexico or New Hampshire. I love my mom."

After I read her notes with her, Sonja dictated: "My mom has three children. She likes roses. She likes to go to the beach with me. I love my mom."

Father's Day: A last-minute project

Panic! It was already Friday and Sunday would be Father's Day. We'd been busy with other projects, and I hadn't noticed that the day was so close at hand until one of the mothers reminded me. What could we do that wouldn't take much preparation?

I remembered that two years earlier one of the students in my class, Melissa, had introduced pop-up cards to me and her classmates — and that the children had really enjoyed trying to duplicate the ones she demonstrated. She had given me a book on the subject as a parting gift. I brought it out, along with the sample cards I'd saved from that time, and asked my students if they'd like to make cards for their fathers. They would.

I suggested that they choose as a subject for their card something their father really liked to do: fish, play tennis, read . . . I had some high-quality paper that was about the right weight for the project.

They enjoyed making the cards. Many of the models were tricky, however, and the children soon learned which of their friends were expert folders and cutters. Some students asked these experts for help; others invented patterns of their own. While they were working I was able to make some interesting observations about their social interactions and their dexterity, tenacity and creativity.

When they were finished, I taught them how to fold paper to make their own envelopes. Panic over. We'd completed the cards in time for the children to have a nice present for their fathers on Father's Day.

Happy notes for the principal: An unplanned undertaking

One morning our principal, Trevor Calkins, came into our classroom after recess to give Kate a "happy note" to thank her for picking up garbage on the playground without being asked. She had presented him with a plastic sack full of litter following his recent announcement of a school-wide cleanup campaign. Although he tried to make the presentation quietly, Kate's classmates took interested note of the event. Most children's etiquette isn't particularly well developed at this age, and some of the other students started protesting: "But I picked up garbage too." . . . "So did I." . . . "I was *with* Kate!" . . . "I helped Art take out the recycling box." . . . "If we do it next recess, will we get one too?"

Trevor was upset: what he thought would be a nice gesture was creating a minor crisis. How do you explain to a group of six-year-olds that life isn't always fair? On his way out he said: "Well, you know, I always pick up papers I see on the ground and no one has ever given *me* a happy note!" He looked pretty unhappy. Poor Trevor.

When the children had settled down, I talked to them and tried to explain the situation. I had Kate put away the award, which was still causing some grief. Then I thought about what Trevor had said and had an idea I felt might turn a difficult situation into a good experience. I suggested to the students that we all make happy notes for Trevor, since he never received any and we all liked him. It would be a nice surprise for him. They thought that was a great idea. We talked about why we liked Trevor and discussed the things he did for us and for the school.

While the students were at work designing the rough drafts of their notes, I cut some pieces of quality paper to a good happy-note size for their final copies. I suggested that they use standard spelling on these notes so Trevor would be able to read them easily, and that they practice their very best printing on the good copy so they would be proud to give them to him.

They brought me their messages after they had decided what they wanted to say and I rewrote them carefully for the children to copy, using proper spelling and punctuation. When the final version was completed and approved, they spent time decorating their work. Some drew pictures of Trevor, some designed elaborate borders and others worked on a variety of colorful scenes. I made a note too.

We finished just before lunch, and Kate went down to ask Trevor to come to our room for a special ceremony. He sat on the carpet with the students, and each child in turn read the message he or she had written, then handed him the happy note.

Trevor took the time to shake each child's hand and appreciate each card. In their excitement about doing something for someone else, the children had forgotten their earlier concern about their own missing happy notes.

Observation

The students were happy to practice the skills necessary to complete this project. Some of the notes were charming, and the children were immensely pleased with themselves:

Chris: "I like your moustache."

Tessa: "You are the best principal I have ever had."

Kate: "Thank you for picking up garbage."

Nicky: "You are a very nice man."

Egg incubation: A planned minor interest study

Every year since coming to this school I've incubated chicken eggs in the spring. The previous year the children and I had studied the subject quite extensively, but I'd decided that this year I wouldn't spend quite as much teaching-time on it. Since we'd studied the life cycle of the salmon in the fall, I didn't want to plan another large block of time in the biology area of the curriculum. I didn't want to give up the project entirely, however, since it's one I enjoy very much and one the students will probably remember all of their lives.

This year Marg and I planned to share the incubation project with our two classes. We placed the incubator in the hall between our rooms and arranged our collection of teaching posters and books so that all of our students, as well as other students in the school, could share in the learning experience. We made calendar charts so the students could see when it was their turn to rotate the eggs and we could keep track of our "due dates." One day we candled the eggs and discarded the infertile ones. We set up our nursery in the sand table.

When the long-awaited day arrived, groups of students took turns watching the hatching activity. It's such an exciting and interesting event!

While the eggs were incubating, the children participated in several short studies involving eggs. In pairs, they studied the parts of store-bought eggs and experimented to see what happens when the whites and yolks are whipped together and separately. They weighed and measured the eggs and sketched them.

Some years I ask my students to keep journals about what they are learning and what they notice about the eggs and chicks, but this year I remembered that they had already done a lot of writing in their science notebooks. I told them I would give them an egg-shaped notebook if they wanted to keep notes, but only one girl asked me for one. However, some of the children drew pictures and wrote, during writing workshop time, about what was happening with the eggs or the chicks.

We divided the hatched chicks between the two classes. We had a good time naming them — using a democratic process, of course. I made up a graph on which we kept track of the chicks' weight. It was fun to gather together each day to weigh them and talk about how they were changing.

After three weeks we sent the chicks home with one of the students who lived on a farm. He kept us posted about their progress and brought one back for a visit so we could see how she had grown. A week later we were shocked to learn that a raccoon had broken into the chicken coop and killed most of the chickens. Monty, our favorite, had lost a leg but was going to live. Some of the children sent him get-well cards.

The museum: An unplanned trip

We were unexpectedly given an opportunity to participate in one of our provincial museum's fine teaching programs, one entitled "Garbage." This wasn't something we were studying, but it's an important subject and I knew the students would benefit from going to the museum and learning from different teachers.

Before our visit we discussed pollution and other important environmental concerns. The children enjoyed the museum experience and the teachers there complimented them on their interest and their good questions. As a follow-up back at school, we had a project day about garbage. As usual, the children completed many different projects. Some, for instance, chose to make posters for the school about caring for the environment.

Parent Appreciation Tea: A tradition

Parent Appreciation Tea has been a tradition in Margaret Reinhard's classroom for years. The event is fun for the children, but the focus is on the parents. She asks her students to think about all the things their parents do for them, and suggests the tea as one way for them to say thank you. This year I decided to hold a tea as well, on a different day from hers because of the large number of people who attend. We'd both need to use the gym and we'd both need equipment from the staff kitchen.

To prepare, my students and I decided together what kinds of things we would like to do for the parents.

- Greet them at the door and find them a good place to sit.
- Read a Big Book together with them.
- Show them how we write and read The News.
- Show them how we can read the thermometer and guess the temperature. (Maybe we would ask them to guess too!)
- Sing a couple of French songs.

- Show them the slides I had taken of our classroom activities during the year.
- Serve them juice, cookies and muffins (and have some ourselves after they had been served).
- Select and enjoy an activity with them. (I hoped we'd perform a dance, but the students voted that down.)

We baked muffins one cooking day and froze them for the tea. The students wrote out the invitations and decorated paper tablecloths for our tables. Some volunteered to bring flowers.

For our bulletin boards I asked the students to draw adult animals with their young. Each student chose a different animal so we'd have a good variety. I insisted that they be very large, the adults at least a meter (3') across. The children looked through our collection of nature magazines and books for ideas. The animals were all to be cut out and pinned up on the boards, with the slogan WE APPRECIATE OUR PARENTS above each. The students used a large variety of techniques and had some very creative ideas. Looking at the artwork, I could easily notice the great spread of developmental levels present in the class.

Many skills were learned and practiced to prepare for this day. The children were totally involved in the project and their parents (and some grandparents) really appreciated being appreciated!

Ryan

My mom could't come to the class tea party so I got a drink. I had three drinks. Then it was time to clean up. I had fun even if my mom wasn't there.

Our class annual: A souvenir of our time together

I've found that my students and their parents like to have a souvenir of our year together, so each year in June I help the class create a "class annual."

The first thing we did was make a list on the board of all the events we could think of that we'd participated in during the year, including field trips, special studies, assemblies, and even regularly scheduled routines like writing workshop and music lessons. Then we consulted our class calendar so we could add things we'd forgotten. When we were sure our list was complete, each student volunteered to write up one or more of the events, as they had when we'd prepared our Traffic Safety Award submission. I helped individual reporters as they edited their work. Some needed to make their writing more interesting by adding adjectives, some needed encouragement to write a bit more, some needed help with sentence structure. As always, I had different expectations for different students.

After everyone had finished editing, I typed each student's paragraph on a different page, including a by-line. Then I gave the originals to the authors for black-pen illustrations. When those were completed, I glued a photograph of the reporter at the top and then photocopied the pages on colored paper and assembled the books. The students were thrilled to see their own pictures on the pages they had written, and we were all reminded of the many different experiences we had enjoyed together during the course of the year.

Family camping trip: An end-of-the-year event

At a family meeting the parents decided they wanted to plan a camping trip for the families of the students in the class, so we made a reservation at a nearby beach campsite. It was easy to arrange: the families were all responsible for their own equipment and most of their own food, although we organized a potluck dinner for the evening meal. Many of the students whose parents couldn't go were invited to join another family, and some families came just for the day.

It was a nice way to end the year. Siblings were included, of course. We went for walks, built sandcastles and spent time in the campground pool. In the evening we enjoyed a communal campfire with marshmallow roasting and singing.

Beach trip: A special event for the primary classes

For a number of years the four primary classes have gone to the beach together for one afternoon in June. It's nice for the students to be able to mix with the children in other classes and for my second-year students to have more contact with their future teacher and some of the students who will be in their fall classes. It gives the parents a chance to get to know the other teachers as well, in an informal setting. We always have enough parents along to ensure everyone's safety and provide sufficient transportation. These events are a lot of fun for everyone, so most parents make arrangements to attend somehow, if they can.

Games Day: A final event

Our school Games Day, held during the last week of school, is organized and supervised largely by the parents. Non-competitive games and activities of all kinds are enjoyed by the students: beanbag toss, water balloons, water slides, parachute play on the lawn, face-painting, informal races and a kickball game between staff members and the senior students . . . At lunchtime the parent group sponsors an entertainer of some kind, and then ice-cream cups are distributed.

The next day is usually the last day of school. After the final assembly, the classrooms are cleaned, personal possessions are gathered, report cards are distributed, and everyone says goodbye for the summer. We've had a good year together.

Four days in detail

How do the daily routines integrate with interest studies? Perhaps the following outlines of four different types of day will help explain.

A "normal" day

Morning

- Welcome, class gathering, chat
- Roll call in French and *Comment ça va?*
- Calendar routines
- The News
- Story
- Simon Says — incorporate exercises
- Writing workshop
    Recess
- Reading time (silent, then shared if they wish)
- Author's Circle (to share writing workshop writing)
- Large-group math lesson
- Small-group math follow-up work
- Review of the morning
    Lunch and lunch recess

Afternoon

- Class meeting/discussion for half-day students
- Independent table time for all-day students (at same time as above)
- Story (all invited to listen)
- Activity time
- Clean-up
- Playground activities
- Sorter material distributed
    Dismissal

A "project" day

(For example, in response to the museum's "Garbage" program — see page 73.)

Morning

- Welcome, class gathering, chat
- Roll call and weather in French
- Calendar routines
- Story
- The News (connect with the project: "Our trip to the museum yesterday")
- A discussion to explain project day (the kinds of things they can do that relate in some way to the project topic)
- Formulation of plans (students remain together until they decide on a project, then disperse, individually or with a friend or two, to begin work)
    Recess
- Continuation of projects (when finished, they prepare for their presentations to the class and discuss their project with me; then they can read until sharing time)
- Sharing time (projects presented)
    Lunch and lunch recess

Afternoon

- Class meeting/discussion for half-day students
- Independent table time for all-day students (at same time as above)
- Short "News" written on the board together
- Several all-day students share projects with half-day peers
- Story
- Activity time (some half-day students may want to do projects)
- Clean-up
- More projects shared with the class
- Playground activities
- Sorter material distributed
    Dismissal

A new "minor interest" day

(For example, tadpoles — see page 42.)

Morning

- Welcome, class gathering, roll call
- Discussion of the minor interest topic (talking about the tadpoles that Ted and his mother brought in; while some students check the library for frog books, others complete the calendar routines; when books arrive we read one, then write The News together, focusing on the topic: "Ted brought in . . .")
- Simon Says — incorporate yoga poses
- Writing workshop (choice of writing about interest topic or another of their own choosing; often less time than usual, so we don't finish before recess)
    Recess
- Finish writing workshop (including reading their work with me)
- Reading time
- Author's Circle (to share writing workshop writing)
- Math activity time
- Review morning
    Lunch and lunch recess

Afternoon

- Class meeting/discussion for half-day students
- Independent table time for all-day students (at the same time as above; one or two students might show and tell the half-day students about the new interest topic — bringing the tadpoles for them to see, for instance)
- Story (one of the other frog books; all students invited)
- Activity time
- Gym
- Sorter material distributed
    Dismissal

A Wednesday

(The "half-day" students stay all day.)

Morning

- Welcome, class gathering, chat
- Roll call in French
- Calendar routines (half-day students do the calendar jobs)
- Story
- The News
- Exercises (led by different students)
- Activity time
    Recess
- Reading time
- Weekly library visit
- Math (group table activities)
    Lunch and lunch recess

Afternoon

- Writing workshop (in writing notebooks)
- Discussion of their writing with me
- Reading time (if time)
- Clean-up
- Sorter material distributed
    Dismissal (1:45)
- (2:00-4:00) Meetings or professional development activities for teachers

AFTERWORD

Where to from here? Even though I've taught for 15 years now, I often think of myself as a beginner. There are several areas I'd like to focus on for improvement during the next few years.

Reporting

One of those areas is reporting. I'm happy with the anecdotal report cards we write at our school now, but they do take a lot of time — hours! I want to look for ways to make this job more efficient. I also think we should involve the students and parents more, not only in the collection of data but also in the actual writing of the report card. I'm planning to incorporate reporting into my student-led conferences. I'll invite the parents to write comments on special forms at each center, both their own observations and their children's remarks about their learning. Then I'll add my own comments to each section after the conference. This two-part form could become a student/parent/teacher report card. It's worth a try!

Questioning

Another area I want to focus on is questioning techniques. Are the questions I ask during our discussions and during our lessons — math, for instance — the best they can be to encourage thoughtful responses from my students and provide stimulation for their own questioning? A new teacher in the school has been working in this area, so I hope to get some help from her.

Evaluation

I would like to improve my math evaluation techniques. I find it more difficult to know where the children are in math than it is in reading and writing, and more difficult to recognize their particular needs. Karen, one of our late-primary teachers, has some good methods I want to ask her about.

Drama

I know that drama is an important teaching/learning tool in a primary classroom. I use it occasionally but I should be using it more. The children love it, and participating in dramatic activities lets them practice many skills. I'd like to have an expert spend a day or two in my classroom to demonstrate a variety of techniques. For me that would be more effective than attending workshops. There are a couple of books on the subject I've been meaning to read as well.

Science

I plan to give my students more opportunities to participate in informal science exploration and experiments.

Storytelling

I want to include more storytelling in my program — by me, by my students and by visitors.

Student counseling

I'd like to become a better counselor, better able to help children with personal home or relationship difficulties. Maybe our school counselor could give me and some of the other teachers some help with that.

Other areas

I would like to integrate more music into my normal classroom activities, improve my physical education program and help my students use the library more effectively.

There's still so much to learn! Just when I think I've learned something, new theories emerge that make me sit back and reconsider. But I don't mind that. To me it's one of the things that makes teaching both interesting and challenging!

A note to new teachers

The career you've chosen is perhaps the most important one in the world. We will never know how much influence we have over the children entrusted to us, but we know from our own memories and from the stories of others that the first teachers and the early school experiences children have are of critical importance.

This is a frightening thought at times . . . but there are several things I try to keep in mind. One is that it's an impossible job: no one can do it perfectly. I will never know how to meet the needs of every child in my class. In the first place, I could never recognize *all* of their needs, and even if I did, I couldn't adequately address the needs of all the children under my care at any one time. What I *can* do is establish an atmosphere in which:

◆ children are accepted for who they are
◆ every child is allowed to achieve success at his or her own level
◆ children feel safe and free to take risks
◆ children's self-esteem is built up rather than undermined
◆ the ideas and thoughts children express are considered important
◆ children learn to love learning

We don't have control over the lives of our students when they aren't with us. All we can do is make school the best place it can be for them while they're there, and check to see if the families of those who appear troubled are in need of any help the school system — through the counselor or the principal — can give them.

In your first teaching position, the most important thing you can do is establish good communication with the parents. Let them know that you consider education a joint home-school effort. Tell them you want to hear from them if something is bothering them or their child, and let them know that you'll tell them if something isn't going well at school, or if there's something they might be doing to help at home. Occasional phone calls or notes home when something is going *well* at school is a good way to establish rapport, especially with the families of children who have had difficulties at school in the past. To them, phone calls have probably come to mean trouble. But if they know you like their child and are trying to help him or her, you'll find their support and understanding easier to foster.

Another important thing is to involve your students in decision-making by allowing them to make choices every day. Children are very understanding and forgiving if you're honest with them, and they're always ready to give advice — usually very good advice! — if you'll listen. If you've made a mistake — frustrated a student by asking him or her to do something that was too difficult, lost your temper and imposed a much-too-strict punishment, given unclear directions that led to temporary chaos in the room — admit it! Talk about it with your students. They know that people make mistakes. They'll be glad to help you out. The frustrated students may suggest more appropriate activities, the disciplined students (who know they've misbehaved) may suggest suitable consequences, the whole class may be willing to reassemble and let you have another try with directions.

> "I'm sorry, Jason. I lost my temper with you and I know that missing recess for a week was too great a punishment. You need to face some kind of consequence for tripping Armando, however, to help you stop doing it. It's not kind and it's dangerous. What do you suggest?"

> "Well, that wasn't very successful, was it? I guess my directions weren't clear. Does anyone have a suggestion about how we can distribute that material so everyone will get some and no one will be trampled?"

Be clear about your expectations. If you expect the children to move slowly and carefully when they form a line at the door before going to the library, show them how it's done and let them practice. Then, if some run to be first in line another day, don't just scold or sigh and shrug your shoulders. Have them go back to their seats and try again. If you want them to put back their toys in a certain way so it will be easy for others to find and use them, make sure that it happens. Don't you do it, and don't let a parent or another child do it. Find the culprits and let them show you they know how it's done!

Take time to establish a set of systems before school begins so your class will be able to run itself, mostly, and leave your mind free to deal with the many curves that will be thrown your way every day. I'm thinking, for instance, of filing systems for your students' work, for the papers you'll be receiving by the handful every day from the office, and for the information you'll be getting from parents. I'm thinking of ways of organizing the papers you'll send home, systems for collecting assessment data that will work for you, and methods of storing materials so they'll be easy for the children to keep tidy. Arrange things so your students can do as much as possible.

Children like to help — it makes them feel competent. And it seems a shame to let all that energy go to waste!

There's no job that is less boring, I think, or filled with more joy than teaching is. Every day is different, every year is different. Each child is unique, and it's fascinating to discover what's special about each one. Each year you'll learn more about how children learn, and each year you'll personally grow in competence and confidence. There are opportunities for fresh starts at every turn — each September, after each holiday, each new day. Teaching gives you access to nonstop learning. If you don't know much about a subject, teach it! You and your students will learn together, you'll be modeling *how* to learn, and you'll share the joy of making new discoveries.

Teaching gives you a chance to form real friendships with colleagues as you work together over the years. The sharing, the support and the advice of fellow teachers is really important, perhaps especially for holistic teachers, and particularly if the administration or parents don't really understand or support the philosophy.

Just realize that you can't do it all the first year . . . or the first five years . . . or ever! You'll become better all the time, through your own experiences: by reading, by attending workshops and conferences, by talking with colleagues, and by simply watching and listening to your students.

Despite all the time teaching takes (as teachers' wives, husbands and children will tell you), despite all the frustrations and disappointments it sometimes brings, I believe, along with a great majority of the teachers I've met, that it's the best choice I could have made for my life. I hope you enjoy your teaching career as much as I've enjoyed mine!

BIBLIOGRAPHY

Forester, Anne D. and Margaret Reinhard. *The Learners' Way*. Winnipeg, MB: Peguis Publishers Limited, 1989.

Forester, Anne D. and Margaret Reinhard. *On the Move*. Winnipeg, MB: Peguis Publishers Limited, 1991.

Johnson, Terry D. and Daphne R. Louis. *Literacy through Literature*. Richmond Hill, ON: Scholastic Canada Ltd., 1987. Distributed by Heinemann in the USA.

Little, Nancy and John Allan. *Student-Led Teacher Parent Conferences*. Toronto, ON: Lugus Publications, 1988.

Picciotto, Linda Pierce. *Evaluation: A Team Effort*. Richmond Hill, ON: Scholastic Canada Ltd., 1992.

INDEX

activity time 30

amaryllis bulb 53

appropriate program 4-5

art 7-8, 39-40, 45-46, 49-51, 54-55, 64, 68, 70, 74

art gallery trip 50

assembly 34, 47

author's circle 29

balanced program 29

basic organization 10-16

beach trip 75

books 26

buddies 32-33, 46, 57

calendar 15, 22

castle study 66-69

chance box 16

Chinese New Year study 65-66

class annual 74

class composition 2-3

classroom environment 6

classroom management 13-16

cooking 44-45, 48, 56, 74

daily schedules 76-77

decision-making 6, 27, 31, 52, 66-67

drama 58

egg incubation 72-73

empathy 5

evaluation 10-11, 14, 19-20, 25, 28-30, 32-34, 38, 41, 51-53, 62, 68

family camping trip 75

Father's Day 70-71

field trips 38, 40, 47, 50-65

French 15, 21

Games Day 75

Halloween 47-48

Hanukkah studies 55-57

happy notes 71-72

house in the street 49

interest studies 17-18

Japanese study 57

Kyla's first year 42-44

library 32

listening center 16

"magnetic students" 15

math 29, 31, 46-48, 53-56, 72-73

modeling 5

Mother's Day 69-70

museum 73

music 31, 65

news writing 22-25, 49

newsletter 16, 50

Parent Appreciation Tea 73-74

parent involvement 12, 19-20, 37, 42-44, 48, 53, 56-58, 65, 70, 73, 75

physical activity 26, 31

plan for the year 35

plans - yearly, daily 12

plant growth 53

polar bear study 62-64

program - daily 21-30

program - often throughout the year 33-34

program - overview 19-20

program - 2 or 3 times a week 30-31

program - weekly 31-33

project days 51-52, 73

reading time 28-29

record-keeping 11-12

review of the day 30

safety studies 36-41

salmon studies 50-52

school community 8-9

science experiments 59-62

sorters 14

student files 11

student-led conferences 52

tadpole studies 42

teachable moments 7

Thanksgiving 45-46

Valentine's Day 64

visitors to the class 36-37, 42, 57

winter concert 57

writers' conferences 32

writing notebook 31

writing together 49, 58-59, 63-64, 68-71, 74

writing workshop 14, 26-28, 31, 58-59